IRISH HOUSES
AND GARDENS

IRISH HOUSES AND GARDENS

FROM THE ARCHIVES OF COUNTRY LIFE

SEÁN O'REILLY

AURUM PRESS

To my family

Designed by James Campus
Series Editor: Michael Hall

Originated by Colorlito Rigogliosi, Milan
Printed and bound in Singapore by CS Graphics

Frontispiece: *Belgard Castle, Co. Dublin, in an unpublished photograph of about 1947 by F. W. Westley*.

Front endpaper: *Details of the nineteenth-century Norman revival castle of Glenstal, Co. Limerick, photographed by Jonathan Gibson*.

Rear endpaper: *The ceiling of the saloon at Carton, Co. Kildare, in 1935, by A. E. Henson*.

INTRODUCTION

The *Country Life* Picture Library holds a complete set of prints made from its
negatives, and a card index to the subjects, usually recording the name of the
photographer and the date the photographs were catalogued, together with a separate
index of photographers. It also holds a complete set of *Country Life*, various forms of
published indices to the magazine and, through the good services of Camilla Costello,
and the generosity of those associated with the magazine, a small archive which
includes the Henson papers referred to in the introductory essay.

Most of the published source material is listed in the introduction and the notices on
the individual houses. John Cornforth's *The Search for a Style*: Country Life *and
Architecture 1897–1935* (1988), Michael Hall's *The English Country House*: *From the
Archives of* Country Life *1897–1939* (1994) and Ian Gow's *Scottish Houses and Gardens*:
From the Archives of Country Life (1997) are all trail-blazing studies to which this book
is greatly indebted and without which it could not have been written. The reader is also
referred to Edward McParland's invaluable 'A Bibliography of Irish Architectural
History', *Irish Historical Studies*, XXVI, no.102 (November 1988).

The Irish Architectural Archive, at 73 Merrion Square, Dublin, keeps photographs
and files on houses, and a bibliographical index on Irish architects, as well as providing
a superb library that includes a full collection of *Country Life*. It is open to the public
free of charge.

HOUSES

The following is a list of the primary articles in *Country Life* featuring the Irish houses
and gardens included in this book.

In the following key, the name of the photographer is given first (where known), then
the date of the article(s), followed by the author.

Adare Manor, Co. Limerick: Patrick Rossmore, 15, 22, 29 May 1969, J. Cornforth.
Ballyfin, Co. Laois: Jonathan Gibson, 13 September 1973, E. McParland.
Beaulieu, Co. Louth: F. W. Westley, 15, 22 January 1959, M. Girouard.
Birr Castle, Co. Offaly: Jonathan Gibson, 22, 29 October 1964, Lanning Roper;
    Jonathan Gibson, 25 February and 4, 11 March 1965, M. Girouard.
Caledon, Co. Tyrone, A. E. Henson, 26 September 1936, M. Jourdain; A. E. Henson,
    27 February and 6 March 1937, C. Hussey.

Carton, Co. Kildare: A. E. Henson, 7, 14 November 1936, B. FitzGerald.
Castlecoole, Co. Fermanagh: A. E. Henson, 19, 26 December 1936, C. Hussey.
Castletown, Co. Kildare: A. E. Henson, 15, 22 August 1936, C. Hussey; Jonathan
    Gibson, 27 March and 3, 10 April 1969, M. Craig, Knight of Glin and J. Cornforth.
Castletown Cox, Co. Kilkenny: A. E. Henson, 7, 14 September 1918, L. Weaver
    (attributed).
Charleville Forest, Co. Offaly: A. Starkey, 27 September 1962, M. Girouard.
Curraghmore, Co. Waterford: A. Starkey, 7, 14, 21 February 1963, M. Girouard.
Glenstal Castle, Co. Limerick: Jonathan Gibson, 3 October 1974, M. Tierney and
    J. Cornforth.
Heywood, Co. Laois: A. E. Henson, 4, 11 January 1919, L. Weaver.
Howth Castle, Co. Dublin: Unknown, 1 July 1916, L. Weaver; A. E. Henson,
    6, 13 September 1930, C. Hussey.
Humewood Castle, Co. Wicklow: Jonathan Gibson, 9, 16 May 1968, M. Girouard.
Lambay, Co. Dublin: Unknown, 4 May 1912, L. Weaver; A. E. Henson,
    20, 27 July 1929, C. Hussey.
Lissadell, Co. Sligo: Jonathan Gibson, 6 October 1977, E. McParland.
Powerscourt, Co. Wicklow: Arthur Gill, 6, 13, 20 December 1946, C. Hussey.
Russborough, Co. Wicklow: A. E. Henson, 23, 30 January 1937, B. FitzGerald;
    Jonathan Gibson, 5, 12, 19 December 1963, J. Cornforth.
Townley Hall, Co. Louth, F. W. Westley, 23, 30 July 1948, C. Hussey.

THE COUNTRY LIFE PICTURE LIBRARY

The Library may be visited by appointment, and prints of any negatives it holds can be
supplied by post.

For further information, please contact the Librarian, Camilla Costello, at *Country
Life*, King's Reach Tower, Stamford Street, London SE1 9LS (*Tel:* 0171 261 6337).

ACKNOWLEDGEMENTS

I must first thank Michael Hall in particular for inviting me to write this book, and for
the benefit of his deep understanding of the entire process. I am also deeply indebted to
Edward McParland for his time and his continuous support and advice from the earliest
inception of this book, and to Ian Gow, for his conscientious guidance.

Numerous other people have assisted in all aspects of the development of the volume,
notably James Campus, whose sharp eye added significantly to the finished work in
numerous ways, and Clare Howell, who co-ordinated activities in the early
development of the material. Camilla Costello and the entire population of the library
at *Country Life* – staff-members Joyce Warren and Olive Waller in particular – were all
unstinting in their assistance and patience.

The text has been improved through discussions with many people, notably, and
again, Michael Hall. The introduction also has benefited from the additional advice of
John Cornforth, whose experience and understanding were essential in the development
of the material; Desmond FitzGerald, the Knight of Glin, whose extensive knowledge
and first-hand appreciation, as ever, enlivened and refined the material; Mark
Girouard, from whom I gained an understanding of the personal perspective; and, once
again, Edward McParland, whose own generous insights helped complete the picture.
It will be obvious to all that I am indebted most to the very authors whose writings
feature in *Country Life*, and hope that my thanks to them register on every page of
this book.

Writing a book on Ireland, designed in London, while resident in Edinburgh,
provided significant logistical problems. It has been simplified by the patient advice
of my wife, Deborah. The assistance of the staff at the Irish Architectural Archive in
Dublin has also proved beneficial, including that of David Griffin, its Director,
Colm O'Riordain, Administrator, and in particular Simon Lincoln, whose helpfulness
continues to rise beyond the call of duty.

Picture Credits: 23 (bottom) from the *Georgian Society Records*, Vol. V., plate LXXIV.

CONTENTS

INTRODUCTION 6

LAMBAY 26

HOWTH CASTLE 36

CASTLETOWN COX 46

HEYWOOD 56

CASTLETOWN 64

CARTON 74

RUSSBOROUGH 82

CASTLECOOLE 92

CALEDON 100

POWERSCOURT 108

TOWNLEY HALL 118

BEAULIEU 126

CHARLEVILLE FOREST 134

CURRAGHMORE 142

HUMEWOOD CASTLE 150

ADARE MANOR 158

BALLYFIN 164

GLENSTAL CASTLE 170

LISSADELL 176

BIRR CASTLE 182

INDEX 192

EVEN today, the role of the country house in the cultural and economic history of Ireland is founded largely on myth and imagination. With the Union at the start of the nineteenth century, Ireland lost its Parliament and, with it, much of its administrative organization. Scotland, after its Union in 1707, had a century of a gradually developing Georgian economy, giving it time to advance its own areas of expertise, in finance, medicine and law. Ireland, in contrast, was thrust into the nineteenth century, a period of unprecedented change, without any clear leadership or agenda. Only its substantial agrarian culture, much of which was centred on the country house and estate, could boast some sense of continuity.

Country house owners became the most coherent social group in Ireland to combine experience in investment with the capital to support it. Though many estates suffered bankruptcy, especially after the Famine, their role within the rural economy, alongside their promotion of an industrial economy, helped shape Ireland's progress. As the popular representative of the rights of the owners at a crucial period in their decline, the voice of *Country Life* was of immense importance.

In a leader of 1 December 1900, *Country Life*, then only three years old, examined again the central issue for the Irish country house estate, the problem of land ownership and distribution. For the magazine, the long list of nineteenth-century legislation had failed to resolve social discontent because it had the unfortunate outcome of putting an unfair price on the land, encouraging people to 'offer more for the right of occupation than it [could] possibly be worth'. The drastic social and economic consequences for all classes of society culminated with the 1881 Land Act, which 'freed [the landlord] from all moral responsibility for his estate' and 'discouraged all efforts on his part to improve it'. *Country Life* accepted that the ultimate problem might lie with the landowners, but saw that the immediate cause lay in inappropriate legislation.

Such comparatively realistic editorial analysis was founded on a philosophy essentially romantic in character. As with so much of *Country Life*'s early coverage of Ireland, this was rooted in its own idealized view of rural society, as expressed in the same leader: 'Our abiding desire is that landowner, tenant, and labourer, the three great classes which go to make rural society, should live together in peace and in amity, in Ireland no less than in England'.

It should not surprise that the magazine's understanding of Ireland was prone to a degree of romanticism. It had been founded by Edward Hudson, a professional publisher, in 1897, and immediately he adopted an editorial policy that is still easily recognizable even today. The English background to the development of *Country Life* has been treated fully by John Cornforth, in *The Search for a Style*, and Michael Hall, in *The*

English Country House in this series, and needs little further analysis here. Hudson's vision of the country house, which shaped the magazine, reflected a popular image of the idyll of *Country Life* fast disappearing under industrial developments and social change. Ireland, remote from the aggressive industrialization invading so much of Britain, could have provided a perfect haven.

Country Life initially presented Ireland in popular terms as a mythic, romantic world, full still of a bygone past, a view surprisingly consistent with the country's contemporary self-image during the Celtic revival. However, for *Country Life* this image was developed in conjunction with its own promotion of social improvement in rural communities. It was to the magazine's credit, and remains so, that it could present at the same time a paean for a disappearing world and encouragement for its improvement.

EARLY YEARS

As early as the second year of the magazine, activities in Ireland began to feature regularly in its pages. The first brief notice of an Irish estate was 'Notes from an Irish Garden', which appeared on 18 June 1898. Mathilda Saunders-Knox-Gore introduced the rich pleasures of her own garden in the west of Ireland, a garden left unnamed but identifiable by anyone interested as that of Beleek Manor, Ballina, Co. Mayo. The pretext for her review was that, because 'so much has been said and sung in praise of English gardens lately', she felt it a 'duty as well as a pleasure to try and describe an Irish one'. This she illustrated with four photographs, though without including a view of the house.

Mathilda's personal approach to her description was in perfect harmony with the style of writing adopted by the earliest contributors to the journal, a variation on the travelogue. 'It is on a bright June day', she writes, 'that I wish to persuade you to stroll with me on the terraces'. She directs the reader from the first terrace, 'close to the drawing room window ... with vases at the top full of bright geraniums and hanging fuchsias', to the second, which has a 'retaining wall ... of grey cutstone, with recesses supported by pillars, against which roses grow in great luxuriance'. Beyond a third terrace may be found the rose garden, about half a mile from the house, Mathilda's 'earthly paradise'. This, she tells us, has 'an old-world look, and one can fancy gaily dressed knights and ladies wandering there centuries ago'. With a sense of transience only too appropriate, and one in keeping with *Country Life*'s own inclinations, she feels that 'in years to come other feet may stand where we do now, and other voices be raised in joy or sorrow when ours are silent forever'. She concludes the magazine's first brief cultural foray into Ireland with the promise of 'a warm Irish welcome should you ever care to turn your steps to the place that has been for years of the greatest pleasure and interest to an old amateur gardener'.

Mathilda's appearance in *Country Life* indicated a few trends that would distinguish its early coverage of Ireland. Distance militated

The so-called 'first terrace' at Beleek Manor, Ballina, Co. Mayo, as depicted in Country Life in 1898.

against sending over staff, so the magazine relied on material being passed on to it. As it was still only establishing its position, for more distant areas such as Ireland it seems natural that its educated readership should provide it with its first items. Such writings, too, would express the concerns of the educated Anglo-Irish landed gentry. Typically, as here, their serious dedication to racing, hunting, fishing and the pleasures of gardening were only occasionally relieved by architectural and more substantial social and cultural concerns.

The next member of the gentry to explore a topic concerning Ireland in the pages of *Country Life* was the claimant to the Earldom of Landaff, explaining his rights to the title, on 21 January 1899. Here the first photograph of an Irish country house appears, the

The medieval vaulting in the guard room at Powerscourt, Co. Wicklow, with the Georgian hall beyond. These historic rooms, later damaged and lost respectively, were only the backdrop to Lord Powerscourt's antler collection.

Landaffs' Irish seat of Thomastown Castle, Co. Tipperary. Lord Powerscourt, of Powerscourt House in Wicklow, followed, with three articles presenting material prepared for his own book, *A Description and History of Powerscourt*, to be published in 1903. Powerscourt reported on his private collection of stags' heads, but the series also included, on 29 July and 12 August 1899, the first views of Irish country house interiors in the magazine. Powerscourt's enthusiasm for his antler collection dominates any passing references to his house, and of his great hall he says only that 'There are sixteen great pillars in the hall, eight on each side, and two pilasters to match at the south end, and on each of these is a very fine stag's head'.

The third item was a report by Lady Onslow on 23 September 1899 about the River Moy in the west of Ireland. As a travelogue, it leads the reader along this famous Irish river, following the history and character of its more notable associations. Lady Onslow considers fishing and recounts tales of the famous Irish 'Chieftainess' Grace O'Malley, a figure associated with most of coastal Connaught. Yet the item is especially interesting in the history of *Country Life*'s Irish coverage in that it incorporates the first illustrated references, if only in passing, to an Irish town, Ballina, and to an Irish abbey, Moyne, and its restoration.

Entitled 'The cabin and the pig', this intriguing view of contemporary rural life in Ireland appeared in 1898, as part of Country Life's exploration of a disappearing and still little-known culture.

Seeing out the century, the daughter of Mathilda Saunders-Knox-Gore, Alice Maude, later of Briscoe House, Bath, published her notice of Achill Island on 30 December 1899. This must have been spurred on by her mother's item, but it was not Alice's first appearance in the journal. On 8 October 1898 a letter from her had been published concerning 'An undistressed Irishman', Pat Murray. She had included a photograph of Pat sitting astride his pony on the same terraces that her mother had illustrated in her article.

Alice's report on Achill opened with an enticing description of the island's Menan Cliffs, with their 'handsome, dark red stone, through

Lutyens's terrace at Heywood, Co. Laois, at the rear of the now demolished house, in an unpublished view by Henson of August 1917, with part of the Victorian extension to the original Georgian house to the left.

which you may venture at low water'. She followed this with the description of cottages at Dooagh, 'unsavoury as picturesque, where the women sit at their doors twisting "sugorns", as the straw ropes are called'. Alice's wider cultural observations are also significant. She notices that such ropes are used to secure 'not only their hay and corn ricks, but the thatch, which in Achill is tied down to the cabin roof and weighted with stones to prevent its being blown away'. Yet, she admits, 'picturesqueness is not everything, and in all the wretched dwellings in which the Achill peasants live, the dirt and discomfort are a terrible item'.

That confused mixture of picturesque admiration, cultural interest and social concern also appears in V. Hussey-Walsh's article, 'Irish Peasantry: Superstition and Progress', which was printed on 29 October 1899. It is at once a critique of, and a swan song for, a vanishing world. 'Old types are rapidly giving way to new', he observes, under the benevolent influence of 'the new co-operative movement ... [which is] doing so much for Ireland'. Between

admiration for Irish loyalty and fear of the thoroughly Catholic nation, Hussey-Walsh relayed the results of his 'quest for local beliefs'. This was undertaken in the company of 'one of the greatest authorities on Irish folklore', though he did not supply a name. Observations of a vanishing world again dominate, such as the fact that nitrate production was rendering kelp uneconomical as a fertilizer, and kelp-gathering, previously a remunerative activity, redundant.

Hussey-Walsh regarded the Irish farmer as 'much more progressive' than his English counterpart. In following the co-operative movement, he recognized his otherwise 'isolated position', and welcomed 'a movement that enables him to make the most of the humble materials at his command'. There was, nevertheless, some sadness at seeing an old world, however unhygienic, disappear: 'The mud hut is giving way to the thatched cabin, and the thatched cabin is being replaced by the slated cottage. The pig is being evicted from his place at the family hearth, and relegated to the sty ... On every side [there is] constantly increasing evidence of the progressive spirit that is abroad.'

Country Life, like many periodicals, recognized the perilous state of Irish society at the turn of the century. More than any, however, it perceived how the country estate, central to so much of the economy, required special consideration. Two articles registered the opposing views of pessimism and, if not optimism, at least relief at progress.

The sad note was provided by the anonymous report on a vacant 'great house' in the west of Ireland, which appeared on 18 March 1899. The house was surrounded by ruinous outbuildings, 'a gas factory, a saw-mill, a magnificent keeper's house ... a huge game larder, enormous stables', all testimony to its economic and industrial importance. The house itself was 'imposing enough', though 'comfort has been sacrificed to splendour'. Inside could be found a 'ballroom and a banqueting-hall fit for any palace', and bedrooms, 'all low and cramped, to pay for the magnificence below'. The house, however, had been vacant for a quarter of a century, 'in Chancery, of course; in the Encumbered Estates Court too, very likely', and with its furniture, 'down to the very grates', all sold. The estate, Cahircon, or Cahiracon, in Co. Clare, was not identified by name, but photographs of the house and grounds appeared, making it the first illustrated notice solely devoted to an Irish country house estate.

The house and entrance gates at Cahircon (or Cahiracon), Co. Clare, in rare photographs of 1899. Its uncertain future was highlighted by Country Life. *Perhaps it was because of this that the house, unlike many similar cases, survives today.*

Farnham, Co. Cavan, with 'hydrants at work', illustrating the progressive developments in Irish estate management encouraged and applauded by Country Life.

A positive development was Lord Farnham's exemplary success at providing a water supply for his house in Cavan, reported on 22 April 1899. Previously, 'the water was drawn from a spring which failed in dry weather'. Lord Farnham developed a small reservoir using a stream on the estate, from which water, filtered through a sand bed, was pumped to a man-made reservoir on an adjacent hill which then served the house. The pressure of water gained by this system allowed for the introduction of fire hydrants. The article concluded with the observation that with such improvements 'the value of many estates would be largely enhanced'.

It was not until the next year that *Country Life* presented its first official notice of an Irish country house, that is, one following the format of the magazine's famous series on country houses and gardens. Christopher Hussey, John Cornforth, Michael Hall and Ian Gow, the last in his recent *Scottish Houses and Gardens*, have all threaded together the main issues involved in the coverage of such houses. The series itself had been developed from a feature that had appeared regularly in every issue since the launch of the title. Already by 1900 the format was well defined, with the text interleaved with high-quality photographs. The new title, 'Country Homes, Gardens Old & New', and the famous headpiece, with castle, topiary and flourished scroll stretching full width across the page, also were in place. This was where *Country Life* would make its greatest contribution to Irish architectural studies.

The first notice of an Irish subject in this series appeared in March 1900. It presented the gardens of Castlewellan, Co. Down, the great triumph of Hugh, 5th Earl Annesley, building on the work of his father. Given the historic importance of this article it is worthy of study in some depth. Probably it originates, as had Powerscourt's own article, in the intended production of a book on the subject, for Annesley his *Beautiful and Rare Trees and Plants* of 1903.

In common with many such early features, the gardens were the focus of interest, though here this was not only due to the interests of the family. The house, being 'comparatively modern, dating from the time of the Crimean War', belonged to that curious middle period, neither old enough nor sufficiently recent to interest *Country Life*'s readership. Consequently the modern Castlewellan was complimented only for being on a site 'chosen with singular felicity'.

As at Beleek, the gardens are presented by way of a guided tour, here led by the Countess. Passing through the sequence of terraces and gardens in a veritable 'path of floriculture', the author visits first the spring garden, which sits along the lake – itself 'one of the largest pieces of private water in Ireland' – and is distinguished by the daffodil 'The Countess of Annesley'. Lying at its foot is the croquet lawn, 'distinctly the venue of the younger generation', while nearby a summerhouse, the Moorish tower, is considered a model of that combination of the refined and exotic typifying the garden folly. 'Built on a rocky knoll, its wide casements of Moorish design overlook the lake, and a little cave below, partially walled in, forms a primitive serving room, whence a small lift can be worked up and down.'

The opening page of Country Life*'s first full notice of an Irish house in its famous series on 'Country Homes'. As yet the content was concerned more with social than historical issues.*

Further along the tour, passing through an iron gate, one meets the ranges of terraces and grassy banks stepping down to the valley, all 'faultily faultless', and pierced by flights of granite steps. From the summer garden one reaches the upper gardens, 'a real sun-trap'. Nearby, surrounded by yews, is 'My Lady's Garden', with its

fountain, 'encrusted with moss and guarded by a fantastic faun'. From here the extensive hothouses, a feature of the estate, and their accompanying exotica may be explored, with a view across the terraces to the deer park concluding the journey. The tour proper is closed with tea, served in the winter garden 'on a massive table of polished native grey granite … surrounded by an army of rocking chairs, which invite us to rest and be merry'. The glass tank, set into the rock-work, contains goldfish and their 'Japanese brothers of the three-tailed variety', replaced regularly because of their 'dreadfully *fin-de-siècle* digestions'.

With this notice on Castlewellan most aspects of *Country Life*'s interests in Irish country living, culture and traditions are outlined. In presentation, however, the articles remain simple and the information cursory, if factual. Here we find no significant history of the garden, no mention that the conservatories, erected before 1872, were by Gray of Chelsea, or that they contained fountains inspired by the Great Exhibition in the Crystal Palace of 1851. That the mansion had been designed in the baronial style by William Burn in 1856 for the youthful 4th Earl, also appears irrelevant. Despite ignoring facts that would secure the continuing historical significance of future articles, clarity and entertainment were recognized as priorities.

The new century would see more academic studies, though still all made accessible through a popular style founded on the techniques already established. The change in tenor was presaged in January 1908 when Sir Edward Sullivan considered not a country house but the 'Library of Trinity College Dublin'. Sullivan, a lawyer, politician and bookbinder with a strong interest in Ireland's cultural heritage, presented a history of the library's collection that included a brief but significant résumé of this key building in Ireland's classical renaissance. He outlined its arrangement and reported on its architect, Thomas Burgh, a figure then 'only recently … rescued from an undeserved oblivion'.

In addition to presenting new research, Sullivan also anticipated later developments by introducing another tool in the consideration of Irish material, the assistance of a local expert. That expertise, fully credited as ever, could be distilled though the wide experience of the *Country Life* author, into an item fashioned in the magazine's authoritative yet popular house style. At Trinity, Sullivan was able to call on Mr Alfred de Burgh, a descendant of the architect, for 'invaluable assistance'. This encouragement for research was to become particularly important in the promotion of the study of Ireland's country houses.

SIR LAWRENCE WEAVER

Country Life developed its appreciation of the wealth of Irish culture very much through its own study of the country house. In a series of articles beginning in 1912, by the staff writer Lawrence Weaver, the magazine laid the foundation for its radical writing of Ireland's post-medieval architectural history. Weaver's study was erratic. He wrote on only four houses, three being selected for their association with the English architect, and hero of *Country Life*, Edwin Lutyens. However, he did succeed in creating an historically significant record of the buildings, as well as presenting an intriguing personal philosophy of Ireland's architecture. The types of buildings, too, were restricted, as Weaver covered two Dublin coastal castles, Lambay and Howth, and two later eighteenth-century classical houses set inland, Castletown Cox, Co. Kilkenny, and Heywood, Co. Laois.

Lutyens's chapel at Howth Castle, Co. Dublin, in an unpublished view of about 1915 by an unknown photographer. It was photographed again in 1930 by Henson, who recorded only minor changes.

There is a remarkable development in Weaver's appreciation, despite such limited experience. Lambay, appearing in 1912, was examined almost exclusively through its documentary history, Continental associations and links with Lutyens, indicating Weaver's comparative ignorance of Irish traditions. At Howth, in 1916, his appreciation was more enlightened. It was enriched not least through recruiting the help of the Irish historian Elrington Ball, who had 'generously placed at [Weaver's] disposal much material'. Doubtless Ball's knowledge of Irish Georgian culture enhanced Weaver's own. The association between *Country Life* author and Irish authority seen here, and prefigured by Sullivan, would reach its apogee in the co-operation between Maurice Craig, the Knight of Glin and John Cornforth in the 1960s.

Weaver's study of Howth might be seen as transitional, for his

reference to Lutyens's work was minimal. Indeed he did not publish views of the architect's own interiors. Lutyens, always careful in the publication of his work, may have encouraged this. However, the tenor of Weaver's article suggested a predominant interest in the original Irish work, particularly as it had been reinstated. The dining room, for example, he described as a 'delightful apartment ... formed by throwing together three little rooms, the panelling of which was carefully re-used'. Weaver also identified some distinctively Irish features, notably the tower corners, with their 'elaborate form of machicolation and the simple four-sided pinnacles ... characteristic of Irish military building'.

Castletown Cox, Co. Kilkenny, registered a new depth to Weaver's interpretation of Irish architecture, one assisted no doubt by the publication of the fifth volume of Ireland's *Georgian Society Records*, the first reference book for classical Irish country houses. The volume appeared in 1913 and, fully credited, it shaped Weaver's notice. For Weaver, and for his successors at *Country Life*, the *Georgian Society Records* would provide an ideal illustrated source, both for original studies and comparative analysis. Indeed, it may be that the book's feature on the house suggested the selection of Castletown Cox to Weaver, though Lutyens himself may again have provided a connection, as he was probably known to the family through the artistic interests of Lady Eva Wyndham-Quin's mother, Lady Mayo.

Regardless of why it was selected, in Castletown Cox Weaver presented a preliminary evaluation of the issues shaping Irish architecture. These were as firm as they were surprising. Castletown Cox, he observed, was not typical of Irish houses, for its architect, Davis Duckart, 'with his Italian training, brought to his work a greater quality of scholarship' than that usually found in Irish Georgian architecture. For Weaver, the 'outstanding fact about Irish architecture is that, after the days of its round towers ... its poverty prevented the development of anything that can be called a native style'. This was because Ireland lacked 'the settled prosperity of yeoman farmers or the industrial classes' that would have spurred a 'tradition of small vernacular building'. When the opportunity arose for new building there was 'no standard of national design to which the official architect could be directed'. Consequently, those who 'could afford to build, imported the architectural manner', and so no independent tradition of Irish architecture could exist. In effect, for Weaver Ireland lacked a successful architectural tradition because of social inequities.

Weaver's authorship of the notice on Castletown Cox is not credited, but his responsibility is not in doubt. The tenor, even certain phrases, reappear in more developed form in his next article, that on Heywood. Moreover, here he acknowledges authorship of the earlier article. With Heywood, which appears in January 1919, the earlier suggestions are constructed into a considerably more coherent philosophy. He is even more harsh in his criticism of Irish architecture, and expresses surprisingly nationalist leanings, particularly considering the unrest of the day. The house, once

The late Georgian dining room, now lost, was the only interior at Heywood to receive detailed coverage by Weaver in his history. His disappointment with the decoration led to an unexpected call for Irish independence in the pages of Country Life.

again, was selected for an association with Lutyens rather than for its intrinsic interest, for Weaver found its architecture unsatisfying. However, this time, seven years after Lambay, he has reservations about this procedure, as 'the employment of an English architect in Ireland gives food for thought, especially as it is in the line of tradition'.

Weaver dislikes the Georgian interiors at Heywood, 'which can only be called "Adam" if we admit a very wide generic use of the word'. In analysing this he tries to identify a typically Irish manner, 'a certain confusion of motif which is characteristic of Irish work of the period'. Observing again that Ireland 'has never produced an indigenous architecture since the days of Celtic art', and making comparison with the rich treasures of Scottish architecture, he can only conclude: 'The reason why a nation so endowed as the Irish with imagination and wide abilities failed to produce anything

distinctive except in the minor art of plasterwork, may be that architecture never develops in a nation that is oppressed. Fine art is essentially an efflorescence of freedom … no nation that believes itself oppressed has any spirit for constructive art, however freely it may express its wrongs in literature and music.'

For Weaver, the lack of Irish self-determination precluded the required investment for the support of the art of architecture. This situation was obstructed further by Ireland's polarized society, which necessarily hindered the development of *Country Life*'s image of a rural social order. Accepting that no simple solution was available, he considered that the arts might unite the parties on all sides, for architecture 'is at least a field of human activity in which all political parties may join; for art has no frontiers, and if Ireland chooses an architecture "for ourselves alone" [a reference to the phrase 'Sinn Féin'], none will complain, so long as the art is reasonable and valid in its own right'.

In an important and positive recognition of the future direction Ireland's political evolution would take, Weaver, on behalf of *Country Life*, hoped that 'the present amazing renaissance in the

The hall at Mount Stewart, Co. Down, photographed by A. Gill in about 1935. This was the first Irish house featured by Hussey not previously reported on by Weaver. Hussey's understanding of Irish architecture was still developing, but his history was exemplary.

material prosperity of Ireland, coupled with some form of political settlement at present unseen, may join in creating a soil in which the plastic arts may take root and flourish'. Given his earlier comments, the settlement necessarily presumed Irish independence. Clearly evident throughout this admonition is the influence of recent Irish writing, from W. B. Yeats's popularization of Celtic Ireland and Robert Elliot's Catholic nationalist essays in *Art and Ireland* of 1906, to the contemporary critical essays in the Irish professional journal, the *Irish Builder*.

THE ERA OF CHRISTOPHER HUSSEY

Weaver's acclaimed successor at *Country Life*, Christopher Hussey, has been identified by John Cornforth as the key author in its history, both because of the longevity of his association with the title, and because of the sophistication of his thought. Weaver's notices

remained rooted in the same broad cultural concerns that had occupied historians in the nineteenth century; Hussey gave a modern stylistic evaluation of the Irish country house, and provided a review of its formal progression and an international characterization that helped identify its 'Irishness'. His considered analysis shaped our historical understanding of the form, and established an international reputation for the type.

As early as 1918 Weaver had identified the need for a more substantial history. In his report on Castletown Cox, he asked whether 'some day, perhaps, an Irish enthusiast in the arts [might] set down a considered estimate of the contribution of his country to the late classical tradition'. The *Georgian Society Records* of 1913 provided histories and lists of select country houses, all tied together by an essay on cultural history revealing more interest in society than in style. Its successor, *Georgian Mansions in Ireland* by T. U. Sadleir and P. L. Dickinson, appeared in 1915, and repeated the formula with more and smaller houses. Its introduction was rather different, being less the history of an art than an architect's history. While it contained an invaluable review of Georgian building traditions, little additional understanding of stylistic developments was expressed, and styles were defined roughly as pre- or post-Adam. Sir Albert Richardson's seminal *Monumental Classic Architecture in Great Britain and Ireland*, of 1914, concentrated mostly on more grandiose architecture. Rather than seeking to define an Irish tradition, he identified consistency across the islands, an essential exercise certainly, but less useful in advancing the understanding of the distinctive tradition of the Irish country house. Weaver's call was not answered substantially for almost two decades, and even then it was fulfilled by another author at *Country Life*, Christopher Hussey.

Hussey came from a stock of artistically inclined English landed gentry, and joined the staff at *Country Life* in 1921. His first ten years saw him develop his own distinctive interests, including the enquiry into a modern 'style for today'. It was his concern for the determinants in a style that encouraged his sympathetic study of the definition and character of Irish architecture.

In the letter discussing Hussey's first contract with *Country Life*, H. Avary Tipping, friend of the family and architectural editor at the magazine, pointed out that payment, consisting of two guineas per thousand words, was inclusive of expenses. As contributors did not get refunds for travelling he recommended that architectural notices might be best arranged in the area in which one lived. Clearly, such an arrangement would militate against extensive research into Irish architecture, and eight years had passed before Hussey turned his attention to Ireland. Then, as so often with *Country Life*'s studies, personal connections paved the way for architectural investigation.

When Hussey first wrote on Ireland, in 1929, it was with some circumspection, examining material already presented by Weaver in new studies of Lambay and Howth. Hussey could update the reader on some issues, such as the introduction of downpipes at Lambay instead of the original unsatisfactory arrangement of gargoyles. He also added a depth of analysis not found in Weaver, though one associated with his wider developments at *Country Life*.

Hussey, for example, devoted more energy to the identification and interpretation of original documents than had Weaver. Through their judicious use he could give a surprising life to the subject. In his discussion of the inventories he examined interiors more often lost than surviving, but these helped piece together the cultural history on the basis of documentation, rather than speculation. Weaver had considered the dining room at Howth 'delightful', and explained it in terms of Lutyens's work. Hussey, adding the perspective of historical documentation, gave a vastly superior evaluation:

To the right of the hall is the present dining room ... described in the 1748 inventory as 'new', and with a picture of the Siege of Buda over the chimneypiece ... By 1751 ... [it] had been subdivided to provide increased accommodation ... The partitions were removed and the dining room given its present appearance in 1910, its panelling stippled white over grey–green. It has a recess on one side formed in the tower that bounds the north side of the entrance front, and the five windows of the room each give a different view. In 1748 it does not seem to have been used regularly for meals, as there were only six 'black Spanish leather chairs on Walnut frames'.

Hussey's initial foray into Irish architecture ended with these two notices, and he did not re-present either of the two other Irish houses covered by Weaver. When he did return, from 1935 to 1937 he directed a series on seven major Irish estates, totalling sixteen articles, which analysed his subject with appreciation and without affectation. Though summary in many details, it contained the first modern history of Irish Georgian architecture. Following tradition, he secured the services of an Irish authority, the historian Brian FitzGerald, to write on two of the earlier houses – Carton, Co. Kildare, FitzGerald's family home, and Russborough, Co. Wicklow. He also called on Margaret Jourdain and G. C. Taylor, specialist staff writers at *Country Life*, to deal with furniture and gardens respectively.

FitzGerald's skills as an historian were exemplary for their date, though his strengths as an architectural historian might be questioned. He incorrectly described the colonnades of Russborough as being in the Ionic order, and unjustifiably remarked that, in comparison to James Gandon's neoclassical masterpieces, 'the houses and public buildings built by Richard Castle', the most prolific early Georgian architect in Ireland, were 'undoubtedly the finer in general design'.

Hussey's own study took form only slowly. His first two notices, on Mount Stewart, Co. Down, of October 1935, and Headfort, Co. Meath, of March 1936, follow the ordinary manner of the magazine's style. Even then the great strengths of his writing are evident. At Mount Stewart he strings together the building's complicated history between literary snapshots of its personal associations, but he makes no comment on characteristic Irish features or their absence. Headfort's history is equally convoluted, despite the availability of a significant body of records. Here the involvement of English architects, notably Robert Adam but also William Chambers, provided a more familiar thread for the author. Yet references to Irish figures are hardly explored, sometimes even overlooked, largely due to his unfamiliarity with the topic. In neither example is there any clear evaluation of the buildings as Irish country houses; Mount Stewart being too complex and Headfort, with its contrast of drab stone exterior and excitable Adam interior, too polarized.

It was with Hussey's history of Castletown, Co. Kildare, in August 1936, that he first formulated his historical and stylistic analysis. As Castletown was 'the earliest fully developed example and, in many respects, the finest' of its type, Hussey considered it appropriate to expand here on the more general issue of Irish Georgian country houses, developing, largely through his own observations, a more substantial study.

Hussey wanted to create a sense of the individual history of Irish architecture, as distinct from that of England. Irish architecture, he observed, 'developed along lines that have only a general reference to English practice', with 'the Palladian convention ... much less universal than Lord Burlington and his confederates succeeded in making it in [Britain], and similarly the influence of Wren'. If one might have reservations concerning some aspects of this sketch, the language rings of the modern idiom of architectural history, immediately confirming the distance between Hussey and Weaver.

The most outstanding characteristic of the Irish house was the 'largeness of scale'. He supported the observation by reference to other houses in the series, citing Russborough, for example, as 'the most extreme instance of this fashion'. For Hussey this peculiarly Irish phenomenon was due to a series of causes, including 'the cheapness of labour, but more particularly to the zest of a high-spirited and competitive oligarchy, inspired by the entire absence of suitable housing to vie in the magnificence and extent of their operations'. Ireland lacked the civilizing connection with Catholic France that had enhanced Scotland's standing in the seventeenth century. Consequently, pre-Georgian Ireland failed to provide modern residences of significance, thereby requiring the largeness of scale evident in Ireland's Georgian architecture.

In a parallel analysis of the issue Hussey rejected the simplistic dismissal of the eighteenth-century development of the large house as 'ostentation … each builder being unwilling to show a less imposing edifice than his neighbour'. Instead he explained it as a response to the need for additional accommodation: 'Establishments were large and accommodation was required, not only for [the owners] (there are large basements in the majority of the houses), but for the servants of the innumerable guests whose coming and going (and staying) was a feature of Irish life.' Few times has the Irish predilection for hospitality been used so sensitively to support the understanding of the architecture.

Hussey considered that the absence of a strong personal influence on early Georgian architecture in Ireland caused it to be distinguished by 'a refreshing individuality of design and detail, the execution of which is almost always admirable'. He also observes that, 'although Ireland had at first no notable architects, there seem to have been plenty of capable craftsmen in the principal cities'. Yet even as he wrote, recent research was introducing new information into the study of the subject, and Hussey was in a position to bring to readers important developments in the study of Irish Georgian architecture otherwise largely inaccessible.

Since the days of the *Georgian Society Records*, the history of Ireland's earlier Georgian architecture had been dominated almost exclusively by the figure of Richard Castle. However, more recent studies, undertaken by Thomas Sadleir in the 1920s, had unearthed a significant new personality in the architecture of the period, Sir Edward Lovett Pearce. Sadleir, in examining a collection of drawings then at Elton Hall, Peterborough, discovered drawings for Castletown by Pearce, thereby placing Pearce at the forefront of classical developments in Ireland. Sadleir presented his study of the architect in the pages of the Kildare Archaeological Society's *Journal* in 1927 but, given the journal's small circulation, it was to be some time before Ireland's finest early Georgian architect won his deserved public acclaim. Despite occasional short articles, such as one in the *Irish Builder* of 1931, it was only with Hussey's notice of Castletown that Pearce gained significant attention.

Hussey's description of Caledon, Co. Tyrone, completed his first series on Irish houses. His concluding remarks summarized the history of post-medieval Irish architecture. They are worth recording here both for their own insight, and for the advance they represent on Weaver's more abstract theorizing. For Hussey, the historical progress takes on a clearer continuity, while the Georgian buildings do not fail to impress:

The houses selected have been very representative of architecture's course in Georgian Ireland, beginning with Speaker Conolly's vast house at Castletown, County Kildare, begun in George I's reign. Richard Castle, the outstanding architect of the century, has been represented by Carton, where the plasterwork is the *chef d'oeuvre* of the brothers Franchini; and Russborough. In the second half of the century the increasingly direct influence of England was noticed at Headfort, designed throughout by Robert Adam; then Castlecoole displayed an unusually complete example of the work of James Wyatt. Before the final additions to Caledon had been made, the classical idiom had been generally abandoned for a Gothic that, historically defensible in England, was as inappropriate as unfortunate in Ireland.

In a few lines Hussey successfully summarized *Country Life*'s view of Irish architecture, and if *Country Life* itself, in the 1960s, proved his dismissal of the Irish Gothic revival wrong, the history is, substantially, recognizable.

In the mid-1940s, Hussey returned to Irish matters, writing on four houses of peculiarly Irish mood and character: Powerscourt, Co. Wicklow; Lucan House and Malahide Castle, both in Co. Dublin, and Townley Hall in Co. Louth. He appears to have chosen these as representatives of major formal issues in Irish Georgian houses. Powerscourt is largely early Georgian fabric, but incorporating a medieval core; Lucan's design is of English origin, transformed by a sympathetic and strong native Irish school; Malahide is a medieval castle with a Georgian veneer; and Townley is a pure example of later eighteenth-century neoclassical design inspired by that great Scottish individualist, James Playfair, but moulded by Ireland's leading native talent, Francis Johnston. While Hussey may have wanted to explore the subtleties of Irish country house typologies, he appears to have come to no clear conclusions on the issue.

Hussey did continue to refine the techniques of the magazine. Following Weaver, he made full use of plans whenever possible, but used them to interpret and explain the history of the house, and not only its arrangement. To clarify the early history of Powerscourt, for example, he produced a splendid précis of the building's history through a diagrammatic plan, probably based on existing drawings, with different phases clearly distinguished. More recent analysis of the fabric has confirmed the accuracy of Hussey's eye.

The architectural analysis in the 1930s and 1940s was complemented by specialist writing on gardens and furniture. In Hussey's series, for the first time in the context of a full study of an Irish house, we find separate articles devoted exclusively to these subjects. Usually these were written, as before, by the magazine's

An unpublished – and uncommon – view of the side of Curraghmore, Co. Waterford, taken by A. Starkey for Mark Girouard's articles of 1963.

regular author on gardens, G. C. Taylor, or by Margaret Jourdain, who provided specialized notices on the furniture.

Jourdain's articles suggest that she may have prepared her descriptions, in some cases at least, from photographs. In discussing the drawing room of Caledon, where the use of mirrors above and below the marble tops opens out the room, she does not express any sense of the relationship between room and furnishings. Throughout the 1930s, however, Taylor followed Hussey's route north from Dublin, writing on the gardens of the great houses, but also preparing separate notices on individual gardens such as the Botanic Gardens in Glasnevin. That he should work closely with Hussey indicates the depth of study considered appropriate to the Irish material. As with the writings of Hussey, the studies by Taylor and Jourdain established an historical context for Irish work, and publicized it to an international audience.

During these two decades, *Country Life* also published separate studies of modern Irish architectural developments. Stormont, the new Parliament buildings for Northern Ireland, built following a classical style, appeared in September 1932. A more dramatic presentation was Hussey's report on Desmond FitzGerald's new airport terminal building at Collinstown, now better known as Dublin Airport. The subtitle to this last, 'How architecture can be modern and classical too', showed that by March 1947, *Country Life*'s response to modern architecture was very reserved.

The researches of two Irish women also appeared in the 1940s. Eleanor Butler, architect and daughter of Ireland's leading traditional architect, R. M. Butler, then deceased, produced two excellent notices on 'The Georgian Squares of Dublin' in 1946. Two years later Constantia Maxwell, historian and first woman professor at Trinity College Dublin, published an important notice on James Gandon, Ireland's leading architect in the second half of the eighteenth century.

The 1940s concluded with the appearance of a masterly review of 'Some Smaller Irish Country Houses', by a young architectural historian from Belfast who would soon reshape the understanding of Irish architecture, Maurice James Craig. Writing in a manner at once both fond and scholarly, Craig looked to the tradition established by Christopher Hussey. Indeed, he responded to a theme recognized by both Weaver and Hussey, observing that 'Social

The Dublin Airport terminal building, designed by a team led by the young architect Desmond FitzGerald, was based on Continental types, and proved that Ireland's modern architecture had much to offer.

cleavages in the great building age were sharper in Ireland than in England'. Being Irish, and familiar with the tradition of the smaller house there, Craig could write most knowledgeably of 'those "middling" houses, which are the backbone of vernacular architecture'. He produced his first review of such buildings, ranging from 'farm-houses to gentleman-farm-houses', on 8 July 1949. That it inspired his masterly work *Classic Irish Houses of the Middle Size*, of 1976, underlines the role played by *Country Life* in supporting, as well as defining, Irish architectural studies.

MARK GIROUARD AND THE 1960s

Edward McParland, in his introduction to his 'Bibliography of Irish Architectural History', published by *Irish Historical Studies* in November 1988, called the 1950s the 'bleak decade' for such research. He did recognize the development of the writings of Craig as a sign of new hope, and the foundation of the Irish Georgian Society in 1958, alongside its publication of the *Bulletin*, as another. However, a third event distinguished Irish studies just at the end of this decade, the publication on 15 January 1959 of Mark Girouard's first article in *Country Life* on an Irish country house. Girouard's mother was Irish, and exploiting his family connections he introduced a new generation of *Country Life* readers to Irish houses, leading the way for a cluster of other, mostly Irish authors. *Country Life* again took on a role of singular importance in the study of Ireland's cultural heritage.

As in earlier years, personal contacts often provided the first spur to the coverage of houses, and for Girouard in particular, family connections with the south of Ireland and friendships with so many of the leading figures in the rapidly expanding Irish Georgian Society, determined the selection of many of the houses discussed by him. However, the pattern of topics in the 1960s well reflected developing interests in historic architecture.

Girouard's first article, on Beaulieu, Co. Louth, was an important study in its own right, but also anticipated a number of future trends. Its pre-Georgian fabric and its smaller scale registered new interests for the magazine, filling out further Hussey's earlier sketches. Yet for all its prescience, Girouard's selection of Beaulieu was practical. The

photographs had been taken by the staff photographer, Westley, more than a decade before, in 1947, and since then had remained on file, waiting for publication. At about this time, Westley had also photographed Belgard, Co. Dublin, a building never actually featured by the magazine, as it came up for sale. Both Beaulieu and Belgard were presented in *Georgian Mansions*, and presumably the photographs had been taken in anticipation of articles by Hussey, inspired by their appearance there.

Girouard's name would soon be most closely linked with Irish country houses of the nineteenth century, a consequence of his wider interest in the architecture and culture of the period. Featuring first Charleville Forest, Co. Offaly, the construction of which opened that century, Girouard went on to bring to light the many treasures of Ireland's later Georgian and Victorian periods. He displayed a special sense of the curious that was in particular sympathy with the subject. He drew attention to the strange furnishings at Birr provided by the estate workshops, items that Hussey might happily have ignored. More typical of the magazine was the glorious, gentle, Regency elegance of the Swiss Cottage at Cahir, Co. Tipperary, abandoned not long after and restored only in recent years, assisted by the magazine's photographs. He analysed the extreme careless-ness that gave Ireland its finest Victorian country house, Humewood, Co. Wicklow; the technological developments under-lying nineteenth-century country houses represented by Tullynally Castle, Co. Westmeath; and work originating in the imagination of a rare Irish genius in architecture, Benjamin Woodward, at Clontra, Co. Dublin. In doing all this Girouard produced a history of Irish country houses in the Gothic style that could stand proudly beside Hussey's history of Irish classical houses. However random in its selection of subjects, Girouard's history was no less important to Ireland's understanding of its architecture than Hussey's.

The strengths of Irish Victorian architecture were well illustrated by Gibson's photographs of Deane and Woodward's Clontra, Co. Dublin (above and right), begun in 1856 for James Lawson QC, with fresco decoration by John Hungerford Pollen.

An extensive school of Irish authors featured in the magazine in the 1960s, spurred on by Girouard and supported by John Cornforth. Assisted by Maurice Craig and the Knight of Glin in particular – eminent authors in their own right – the history of the Irish country house begun by Weaver, and ordered by Hussey, was refined and, where necessary, rewritten. Russborough reappeared as Cornforth's first inspection of an Irish house, carrying with it all the strengths that would characterize the studies of the 1960s, not least the busy help of Irish authorities. The increased respect for documentation, the more sophisticated history within which Irish traditions might be understood, and a continuing concern for issues of conservation, together registered new heights in the analysis of the subject.

The Knight of Glin, for example, as part of his postgraduate studies of the Irish Palladian tradition, published his reconsideration of Castletown Cox from 28 September 1967. He transformed Weaver's descriptive history of the house into a comprehensive examination of the work of its architect, Davis Duckart, as once again *Country Life* became the forum for some of the best Irish architectural studies of the decade. Perhaps the single most important notice in this energetic decade was that on Castletown, Co. Kildare. Writing over three articles from 27 March 1969, Craig, Glin and Cornforth re-presented the history of the house. Already the magazine's archives were proving invaluable, as one of the 1930s photographs was used to show the original interiors, by then sadly bereft of their contents. At the same time, the authors celebrated the rescue of the house by Desmond Guinness and the Irish Georgian Society.

Mark Bence-Jones, during this period, contributed a series of important and innovative articles on Irish towns, a tradition presaged by Lady Onslow's passing reference to Ballina in 1899. He also pioneered studies on lost Irish country houses, looking in some detail at their culture. His concern for the society of the house in the nineteenth century encouraged his own interest in Victorian country houses, and so another thread of studies by *Country Life* of Ireland's Victorian heritage commenced.

The magazine also gave extensive support to conservation issues in Ireland from this time. It raised concern for planning travesties in the capital and elsewhere, as they led to the ravaging of a national heritage for the short-term gain of a powerful minority. Often these were featured as part of an Irish number, in which *Country Life* presented a sustained review of all matters concerning Ireland. Whether inside or outside an Irish number, *Country Life* celebrated the few successes and the lonely initiatives of conservation groups too often castigated in their own country for asking for the intelligent deployment of a national resource.

Country Life's authors continued writing into the decades after the 1960s, developing further the study of Ireland's architectural history all the time. Their numbers were enhanced significantly by the addition of new figures. Alistair Rowan, briefly a staff writer, was concerned largely with his native Ulster. Edward McParland's

studies in later Georgian architecture helped discover new treasures. With advances in Ireland's architectural appreciation, new publications appear and old respected titles evolve, as the Irish Georgian Society's *Bulletin* becomes its retitled journal, *Irish Architectural and Decorative Studies*. However, *Country Life* may be recognized easily as the single most important publication of this century in promoting the understanding and protection of Ireland's post-medieval architecture.

Henson's view of the porte-cochère *at Heywood, by Thomas Drew, was not published, but it remains an invaluable record of this part of the now demolished building.*

PHOTOGRAPHY

Country Life has also made the most important photographic record of Irish country houses this century. Indeed, to many its writings are less immediately interesting than the photographs. These have a special significance as records, often of buildings now lost or of interiors dispersed or rearranged. The magazine's views of Heywood, of Powerscourt and of the early furnishings at Castletown all have a great importance in recording aspects of Ireland's cultural heritage now lost for ever. Records of Russborough over nearly thirty years, from abut 1935, show the house gaining a whole new magnificence. At Lambay we see a house also in transition. Here it is being eased into the twentieth century by the caring hand of a sensitive architect, Lutyens, and by the conscientious nudging of patrons aware of the heritage in their care.

The photographs have a special importance also because *Country Life* has always set high standards, demanding an uncommonly consistent professionalism. However, at the start of this century, professional architectural photography was an arduous discipline. A country and culture largely unknown to the photographer, such as Ireland, compounded any difficulties, and only in the second decade of this century did *Country Life* send staff photographers to Ireland. Prior to that time the source of images is uncertain.

We may presume that the views of Beleek were produced by a member of the family, as they bear the trademarks of the 'snap' of an amateur. The illustrations to the article by Lady Onslow are credited to P. and S. Knox Gore, while those to Hussey-Walsh's report are by W. G. Knox, all suggesting the possibility of a more general connection between authors and photographers. Such a proliferation of photographic technology need not surprise; from 1888 the Kodak camera was available, with its slogan of 'You press the button, we do the rest'. Its reliable quality ensured that numerous photographs could be supplied to the magazine, not only of gardens, but also of pets, horses and hunting trophies. Even Lady Annesley was described by *Country Life* as having a 'ready camera'. The photographs of Castlewellan and Powerscourt may be associated with the wider publishing programmes envisaged by the two families, who simply submitted photographs to the magazine.

The photographers for Weaver's first two Irish articles, unfortunately, are unknown. They need not have been staff photographers, though the quality and style of the images suggest nothing to contradict it. John Cornforth, among others, has reviewed the major figures in the early history of the magazine's photography, and no likely candidate can be identified. A. E. Henson, principal photographer from his appointment in 1916 until his retirement in 1957, need not have had any responsibility for these buildings, but he did photograph the vast majority of Irish material before 1960.

For Henson, whose perfectionism was legendary, a good photograph was effected less through the selection of the decisive moment than through arduous preparation. As Cornforth observed: 'Elaborate progresses had to be arranged for him ... the electric current had to be checked in advance because it was so varied, if not non-existent; the household had to be on hand to pull blinds as required and move quantities of furniture; lawns had to be re-mowed if the lines ran the wrong way, and branches – and even once a tree – had to be felled when they were in the way of his composition.'

Henson's work was complicated further in Ireland, as recorded in a surviving diary, which covers the short period after his official appointment to the magazine in 1916. The diary was deposited recently with the library of *Country Life* through the courtesy of his daughter Maudie. Its entries show that he was the previously unidentified photographer of Castletown Cox and Heywood. These were among the first projects after his appointment, and may be studied in some detail.

The visit to Ireland was first broached on 30 July 1917, during the latter part of the First World War and not long after the Easter Rising of 1916. Hudson, in a typically abrupt announcement, asked that Henson be in Ireland within a week. As this was not possible, the matter was postponed until August when organizational details, complicated by the war, were more in hand. By mid-August, as his diary records, Henson had received communication from the 'Commander-in-Chief of the Forces in Ireland saying he did not object to his photographing the various houses'. Henson also arranged that, given the dangers of his journey to Ireland, *Country Life* insure him for at least two thousand pounds, and not the one thousand originally suggested.

Travelling, on its own, was an ordeal. Departing for the ferry on Thursday 16 August at 8.25 a.m., he arrived in Holyhead at 2.20 p.m. to cross in the *Leinster*. The ship, Henson notes in his diary, later was 'sunk by submarine'. He arrived in Kingstown, now Dun Laoghaire, at 5.40, and travelled to Kingsbridge, now Heuston station, to book into the College Hotel. 'Nearly lost my own bag while booking this', he wrote in the diary; 'someone moved it and took label off'. In central Dublin the evidence of the Easter Rising was still strong, as he reported that 'All the buildings from O'Connell Bridge to just past [Nelson's] column are all down (on right hand side)'. The day concluded with the sending of a wire to his wife, Maude, telling her of his safe arrival.

Heywood in Co. Laois, nearly sixty miles from Dublin, was his first stop. He left Kingsbridge by train at 9.15 a.m., changed at Maryborough for Abbeyleix, from where he was collected by car, reaching the house about lunchtime. After a quick look around the house with Sir Hutcheson Poë he took lunch and set about work, taking three exterior views and two interiors over an afternoon that was 'sunny at times and very windy'. Unfortunately, as might be expected, the weather did not hold for long, and on Saturday all he could photograph were interiors – five negatives – and 'an old Punch Bowl that belonged to The Hell Fire Club'. Mixed weather on Sunday, with patches of brilliant sun, allowed him to squeeze in ten more shots.

At Heywood, as elsewhere, it is clear that Henson's critical eye for features was greatly valued by the magazine, especially when he was working in Ireland. Indeed, there is nothing in his diary to suggest that there were any specific instructions from Weaver for these Irish shoots. Looking at the collection in Heywood, he judged Sir Hutcheson Poë to have 'some very good foreign stuff, not much good old English or Irish'. Left unrecorded, this was to be, in effect, the final judgement by the magazine on the matter.

By Tuesday 21 August, the weather was beginning to depress Henson: 'Wind, wind, wind, nothing but wind all day long and rain at times'. He struck up a friendship with Hugo, Sir Hutcheson Poë's son, who confided that 'he did not like a lot of people' as 'he stammers badly and gets excited'. By Saturday Henson was 'Absolutely sick and tired of this weather'. On the following Thursday he writes that 'the servants are firmly convinced that I am the cause of the weather being bad and that it will clear if I go away'.

Eventually, apparently agreeing with the servants, he left Heywood to visit nearby Ffranckfort Castle, near Roscrea, an idea probably inspired by the writings of its most famous resident, the author T. W. Rolleston. This was only to provide further disappointment as Henson considered it 'no good' as a feature, it being 'not kept up, over-grown with ivy etc. and the back ... simply a farmyard, or more correctly, a stable yard'. After another unproductive visit, this time to Holy Island, again undertaken on his own initiative, he left Roscrea for Castletown Cox.

Henson arrived at Castletown Cox on Monday 3 September at 2.40 p.m., with enough time to capture three interior views. As the weather remained dull, he concentrated on interiors until Wednesday when, it being a nice day, he took sixteen outdoor shots. Unfortunately, a wire from Hudson, preserved with Henson's papers, came that day, asking that he return to London as soon as possible on Government business of the utmost secrecy. Never one to miss an opportunity, Hudson followed his compliments on Henson's recent work with a request that he photograph Lismore Castle, the Devonshire seat in Waterford, should time allow. Time did not permit, and by the following week Henson was back in London secretly photographing Chequers before its presentation to the nation.

The complexities of travel to Ireland were not simplified with the coming of independence in the following decade, for the bureaucracy only increased. Henson's papers show that, for the trip in the mid-1930s, Hussey was in communication with the Secretary to the High Commissioner for the Irish Free State to arrange for the duty-free transport of the equipment. He also carried a shrewd letter of reference from Hudson which stated that the photographer was in Ireland to record 'gardens, architecture and the beauties of Ireland generally for ultimate publication in *Country Life*, and to encourage tourists to visit the country'.

Two other names may be linked with the early phase of Irish photographs: Arthur Gill, best known for his series on Delhi, who photographed Balawley Park, the Botanic Gardens, Lutyens's National War Memorial, all in Dublin, and Powerscourt, Co. Wicklow, as well as numerous gardens; and F. W. Westley, who photographed Beaulieu, Co. Louth, Belgard Castle, Malahide, Co. Dublin, and Townley Hall, Co. Louth. Both followed so closely the exemplary style of Henson that their work appears largely indistinguishable. In the 1960s Jonathan Gibson and Lord Rossmore were the most prolific photographers for the magazine in Ireland.

The wider impact of *Country Life*'s photographs on Ireland in the first half of the century deserves special consideration, though their relevance to the architectural profession remains unclear. Certainly, as it was an English magazine, particularly one prone to promoting English architects, Irish architects viewed it with some circumspection. As Sean Rothery observed in his *Ireland and the New Architecture*, of 1991, *Country Life* was mentioned only in passing in the *Irish Builder*, the trade journal, and then usually for its reports on Lutyens's work in Ireland. Indeed, perhaps the most explicit adaptation by an architect in Ireland of *Country Life*'s images was that by Lutyens himself. He copied the newel posts on the east staircase at Astonbury, Hertfordshire, featured on 26 March 1910, in his Lambay staircase.

In both England and Scotland the magazine's photographs often have a particular significance for recording people's tastes in country house interiors. However in Ireland, as sales depleted or destroyed the rooms, the photographs are often the only significant record of the contents, and so gain a remarkably important role. They also offer intriguing insights into the histories.

The changing image of the interior is well explained in the contrast between the hall at Castletown Cox in about 1913, as presented in the *Georgian Society Records*, and Henson's view taken in 1917. In the earlier view the flurry of soft furnishings, animal skins, plants and screen, give the room a natural and genuinely homely character, although they distract from the plain grandeur of the architectural space. Henson captures a space severely characterized by an uninterrupted sweep of floor and ceiling, eased only by the furnishings barely visible in the confusion of the earlier photograph.

Above: *Two visions of the hall at Castletown Cox, Co. Kilkenny:* (top) *as ordered by Henson in 1917, and* (above) *the more ordinary – and realistic – cluttered view that appeared in the* Georgian Society Records *in 1913.*

Left: *An atmospheric view by Patrick, Lord Rossmore, of part of the south front of Adare Manor, Co. Limerick, showing P. C. Hardwick's work of the 1850s, with the Wyndham tower behind.*

As representations of real Irish interior arrangements, Henson's views must be treated with some circumspection. His photographs were artistic records first, and social documents only second. Yet it is especially interesting to observe the degree to which he alone was responsible for the appearance of these rooms. In his diary he refers to complaints passed to Hudson from an owner concerning the extent to which he moved the furniture, and Hudson's surprise and reprimand. In his defence, Henson noted that the procedure only made his work more difficult, but he continued to compose his interiors as carefully as he did his exteriors.

Comparison of interiors is endlessly stimulating, and perhaps the most moving concerns the interiors of Castletown, Co. Kildare. As photographed by Henson in about 1935, it was replete with fascinating furnishings. In about 1969 it was recorded by Jonathan Gibson, almost bereft of contents as the Irish Georgian Society did not have sufficient funds for their rescue. Glin, Co. Limerick, is a wonderful Georgian Gothic castle with a more successful history. Featured by Girouard in 1964, after being photographed by Alex Starkey, Henson's successor as staff photographer, at present the house is being recorded for another notice in the magazine. It is a rare example of an Irish house in which the interiors have been enhanced by new contents and restoration, while also confirming the continuing links between Irish houses and *Country Life*.

This book is not a document of a lost culture, but a celebration of a culture that in some special places very much lives on. Yet because of its very rarity, it is deserving of special consideration. Whether one admires the photographs of vanished Irish houses, or simply enjoys those few still in some way representative of this profoundly significant aspect of Ireland's traditions, or even if one prefers the rigorous analysis supporting its eminently readable histories, we may happily acknowledge our gratitude to all concerned with *Country Life* throughout its history.

Left: *The drawing room at Russborough, Co. Wicklow, as it appeared in Henson's photographs of about 1935, when the house was the seat of Captain Denis Daly, and before its rearrangement as the home of Sir Alfred and Lady Beit.*

Above: *The hall at Glin Castle, Co. Limerick, the seat of the Knights of Glin, photographed by Starkey in about 1961; like Russborough, it was one of the few Irish houses to improve over the years.*

ONE

LAMBAY

Co DUBLIN

When Cecil Baring, later Lord Revelstoke, bought Lambay Island in 1904 it was intended first as a 'desert island', its derelict castle being
little more than a picturesque motif. The island's many rugged beauties, however, quickly persuaded him to adapt it as a home,
so in about 1905 he called on Edwin Lutyens, proven master of castle renovation, to reconstruct the building and provide a garden setting.
Through Lutyens's involvement, Lambay became the subject of the first serious study of an Irish house to appear in *Country Life*.
In 1929 it reappeared, opening Christopher Hussey's series of Irish studies.
Strategically situated on the coastline some three miles from the capital, the square mile of rock and ridge known as
Lambay Island has had a long history fraught with stories of banditry and intrigue.

Pirates were naturally drawn to a site of such significance to marine traffic, and their shrewd exploitation of its natural geography had, by the 1400s, made it 'a receptacle for the King's enemies'. Such dangers emphasized the importance of securing it for the public good. In these times security required a castle, and one was proposed in the late fifteenth century, and perhaps built, by John Tiptoft, Earl of Worcester and Lord Deputy to Edward IV. This may have formed the core of the castle still surviving when Baring purchased the island.

Weaver's first article on an Irish house already showed clearly his concern for disposing of unauthenticated traditions. Among those he corrected was the presumption, promulgated in Samuel Lewis's *Topographical Dictionary* of 1837, that the island was granted by Queen Elizabeth to Archbishop James Ussher, a figure famous for dating the creation of the world to 4004 BC on the basis of a chronology of the Old Testament. Weaver pointed out that the island was in fact held by Ussher's cousin, William. Despite many vicissitudes, Lambay Island remained in the possession of the Usshers from 1551 to 1804, from which time no significant work was done on the castle until the arrival of Baring.

Weaver's concern with the true history of the architecture at Lambay was not assisted by his study of its recorded history, any more than this was to help Hussey in 1929. Indeed the evaluation of the fabric, always such a valuable asset to the *Country Life* authors, was of rather more use in assessing this particular building. The most distinctive feature of the medieval castle was the acute angles to the corner bastions, which gave them an arrowhead profile and improved defensive coverage. This was

Preceding pages: *The east end of the sitting room in 1929, with a view to the house from the bastions, all as photographed by Henson.*

Left: *Lambay in 1912, with the medieval castle on the left, and the new service wing, with its low pantiled roof, on the right. Lutyens replaced the sash windows in the castle with casements.*

Above: *The front, or west forecourt.*

characteristic of castles of the Renaissance, and for Weaver this
suggested, most reasonably, the unlikelihood of an association with
Tiptoft's fifteenth-century work.

Hussey, when writing his history, was still unfamiliar with Irish
work, and appropriated Weaver's evaluation, and even in places his
phrasing. He did argue that an earlier fabric might be contained
within the later building, referring especially to the hall. However,
he was more emphatic in asserting 'a wholesale reconstruction late
in the sixteenth century at the earliest', an estimation with which
modern historians would, with some additional refinement, agree.
The frustration of integrating documentary and archaeological
evidence, so often a challenge for the architectural historian, is
acknowledged by Hussey's remark on its contrariness; he observed
that 'relatively complete records of that [sixteenth-century] period
… make no reference to so important an undertaking'.

By the time of Lutyens's arrival much original fabric had
deteriorated, and he was required to rebuild in part, though he
retained triumphantly the ancient mood. A new service range was
necessary, discreetly located off a corner of the castle and set into
the ground so as not to dominate the main castle. Lutyens also
ensured the prominence of the medieval fabric by deciding not to

Above: *The entrance hall leading to the dining room* (top)
in photographs of 1929. The latter, shown in an
unpublished view, retained its original vernacular-inspired
furniture.

Right: *The dining room leads to the new staircase hall.*
Though recorded in 1912, in the view shown here, it did not
appear in Country Life *until 1929. The staircase connected*
the first-floor bedrooms and the raised ground level at the
rear of the castle.

IN HOC THALAMO
LUCEM ADHT
CALYPSO
BARING
10. OCT. MCMV

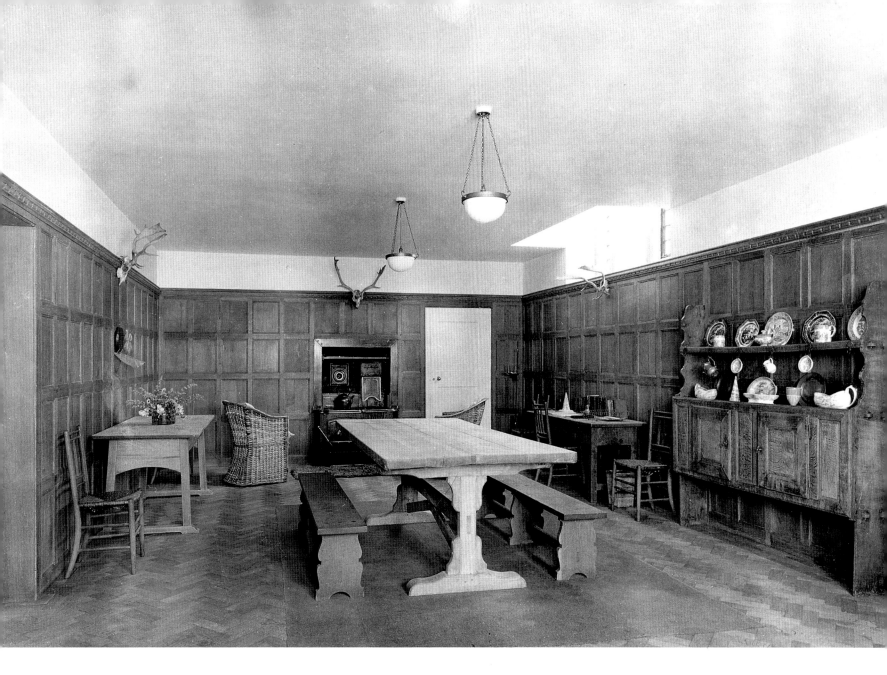

repeat the leitmotif of the original – its stepped gables – in the new work. Instead he used steep sweeping tiled roofs broken by dormers, gables and stacks.

Lutyens did need to provide suitable facilities within the surviving ruins of the castle, the most basic of these being a staircase. Curiously, the original castle fabric did not possess internal access to the upper floor, so Lutyens inserted his in the space between the bastions at the rear of the building. He linked these two with a sequence of three cross windows broken by the arched doorway leading to the staircase. The new arrangement is a typically imaginative piece of intervention by Lutyens, as it performs a number of functions with appropriate efficiency. It gives access not only to the bedrooms on the upper floor, but also to the raised ground at the rear of the castle, and it connects to the underground service passage to the kitchen wing.

Reception rooms also needed to be provided inside the ruins, and again it was to Lutyens's credit that he succeeded in creating an imaginative variety of shapes and spaces without intruding on the individuality of the building. Perhaps most surprising is the provision of two entrance halls, one in each of the corner bastions

Left: *As in this bedroom, the castle's interiors were severe, usually with scrubbed elm boards and whitewashed walls, enlivened by grey stone with occasional inscriptions.*

Top: *The most elaborate interior was the panelled servants' hall, set in the new wing (above). The photograph was by Henson, but it remained unpublished, and the hall was not mentioned by Hussey. Henson's view of the courtyard highlights Lutyens's complex exploration of levels.*

of the entrance front, and each with its own door. The sitting room, reached only after passing through the central dining room and staircase hall behind, is in the corner adjoining the service wing. Due to the need for reconstruction of this corner Lutyens was more free to open out the architecture, without actually intruding on surviving original fabric. Here he introduced a pointed stone arch linking the section of the room in the original bastion with that part set between the bastions. Lutyens topped this range with a hipped roof – an informal nod to the detailing of the service wing – and square battlements – a more formal bow to the stepping in the original gables, seen across the view of the north court.

Drawings in the University of California suggest that the gardens were laid out by Lutyens working with Gertrude Jekyll, whose characteristic use of informal planting to soften the hard

Left: Lutyens's stone newel staircase connects different levels in the kitchen wing. This photograph, of 1912, captures perfectly the sense of pure volume found in the best of his work.

Below: The north court in 1929, with the new wing to the left. The part of the castle seen to the right was extensively remodelled by Lutyens. Hussey considered the Dutch inspiration of the new, pantiled domestic roofs to be especially sympathetic to the stepped gables of the fortified old castle.

lines of the architecture dominates the immediate setting. Always intended to occupy all sorts of crevices, hanging creepers and bright distracting borders jump between different levels and spaces in a fashion recalling the arrangement of the house. So between the kitchen garden, situated to the south, and the Revelstoke memorial nudging into encircling ramparts on the north, lie the service yards, the wild garden and bridged brook, orchard and lawn. Together these capture perfectly the unity of humanity and nature, and epitomize Jekyll's integration of architecture and garden.

The complex interweaving of old and new in the architecture of the castle was continued into the topography of the island. Using walls, rails, ramparts and bastions, and combining suggestions from the island's entire architectural history – from placing classical mouldings on piers to converting a cowshed into a pergola – Lutyens created a complex that was at once comfortably familiar in its setting and wholly new. Lutyens was also responsible for works concerning an array of other buildings on the island, including workers' cottages, the old Catholic chapel on a hill, the memorial, and the White House, a low harled house built in the 1930s for Lord Revelstoke's daughter. The entire complex survives today mostly in its original form.

TWO

HOWTH CASTLE

Co DUBLIN

It was the recent association of Edwin Lutyens with Howth Castle that first attracted the attention of Lawrence Weaver, rather than its survival for more than half a millennium as the residence of the St Lawrences, Lords of Howth. Yet Weaver's admiration for the castle impressed itself on him to such an extent that he did not illustrate Lutyens's new interiors – of chapel and library – but only his renovations of the old.

Howth Head is a peninsular extension reaching out from the north of the city of Dublin into the Irish Sea, with a view to Lambay Island. It rises high in the skyline, a proud and somewhat isolated district in which the estate of Howth Castle still plays a role today uncommonly dominant, especially considering its proximity to the capital.

Even more surprising, in these circumstances, is the survival of so much of the historic fabric of the castle. This rare state may be explained in part at least by the tradition that Howth Castle is the oldest inhabited house in Ireland. The other reason is Lutyens's careful remodelling at the start of this century.

Howth Castle's earlier interiors had little of the immediate grandeur that Weaver might have expected in one of Ireland's most historic seats, for it had been extended fitfully from a medieval keep at a number of stages, the most recent of which was the building of Lutyens's new tower. This tower picked up many of the motifs distinguishing the earlier fabric, from its irregular massing to the use of stepped battlements with pyramidal pinnacles, all moulding it into the meandering fabric of the earlier buildings. Throughout, Howth Castle presents the same unostentatious modesty, here born of an antiquity comfortably worn.

It is Lutyens's selective retention and sensitive recovery of surviving original fabric from a variety of eras that distinguishes his work at Howth. The entrance hall, at the head of a wide flight of stairs, displays best his ability to empathize. While the photographs, by an unknown photographer and by Henson, convey his success, Weaver's summary clarifies the architect's methodology: 'The general work of reparation in the interior revealed in the hall fireplace an old elliptical arch which enabled the original open hearth to be used once more. Above it Mr Macdonald Gill had

Preceding pages: Lutyens's arched loggia which hides behind the entrance front, with the pond, a remnant of the formal Renaissance gardens and the medieval, probably fifteenth-century, gatehouse, all photographed by Henson.

Above: The chimney-piece in the entrance hall was developed from existing Georgian and Victorian features, and medieval fabric recovered during renovation, providing an enticing mix of styles typical of Lutyens's restorations.

Right: Henson's unpublished view shows the dining room after its reinstatement using surviving eighteenth-century panelling, an important early example of Irish Georgian revival.

painted, under Mr Lutyens' direction, a charming conventional
map of Howth and the neighbouring sea and a dial which records
the movement of a wind gauge.'

The dining room required a more invasive procedure, but one
carried out, as might be expected of Lutyens, with the utmost
regard for the character of the surviving fabric. Returning to
something like its original form an early eighteenth-century room
that had been subdivided soon after its construction, Lutyens
managed to create a convincing reinstatement of an Irish early
Georgian room cobbled into castle fabric. The attempt was
assisted, no doubt, by the models provided in the charming
contemporary survivals already on hand in the castle, notably
the panelled walls to the timber staircase.

The drawing room, recorded in about 1915 by an unknown photographer (left)
and by Henson in about 1929 (above), *was left largely untouched by Lutyens.*
Above the vigorous chimney-piece is a view of the castle painted in about 1740,
soon after its extension. The soft furnishings creeping into the borders of the
earlier view do not appear in Henson's, marking a whole new taste.

A more elaborate manifestation of an appealing, provincial Irish
character was on hand in the chimney-piece inserted by Lutyens in
his new library, as if in respectful admiration for its idiosyncratic
integrity. Whether the inspiration of Lutyens himself, or of his
patron, it made itself the centrepiece of the new room. Lutyens's
studied roughness – with too-big beams banging into walls – fails to
do anything more than form a backdrop to the vivacious confidence
of the genuine early Georgian marble chimney-piece. Of Lutyens's
two new main rooms, it was the quirky personality of the library,
rather than the austere purity of the chapel, that reflected best the
character of the original interiors.

Strictly speaking, Weaver was not the first to write on Howth in
Country Life. Among the tales related by Lady Onslow in her
discussion of the River Moy and the west of Ireland, referred to in
the introduction, and its links with the famed Irish chieftain Grace
O'Malley, she recounts O'Malley's visit to Howth Castle, in search
of provisions after returning from London. Failing to receive a
reply to her knock, as the family were at dinner, O'Malley

kidnapped Lord Howth's heir who had been playing on the beach. She did not return him to the family until she had extracted a promise from Howth that 'never again should his gates be closed against guest or stranger during dinner time'. That this tale is repeated, with either modification or elaboration, by both Lawrence Weaver and Christopher Hussey in their notices on the castle, confirms the continuity between the first articles on Irish culture in *Country Life*, and those of the following century.

The castle itself rests on foundations that, according to some traditions, go back nearly as long as the St Lawrence family in Ireland. Almeric St Lawrence founded his family's fortune on his success in the Norman invasion, as a soldier fighting alongside his brother-in-law John de Courcy. Almeric's grandson confirmed his family's title to Howth, and the St Lawrences maintained and improved their fortunes as Lords of Howth even into the present century. The castle reflected the success with which the family developed their position – neither advancing so fast that the castle might need anything more than judicious improvement, nor losing political face and forfeiting it. The death of William, 4th Earl and 30th Baron, in 1909 saw the extinction of the line. The estates devolved on a nephew, Julian C. Gaisford, who assumed the additional surname and arms of St Lawrence. It was he who was responsible for calling on the talents of Lutyens to upgrade the castle.

The castle confronting Lutyens was a complex amalgam of phases of building and rebuilding, the detailed history of which remains uncertain to this day. The structure visible in the early twentieth century had originated with a tall and broad medieval keep situated to the south, or left, of the present entrance range. The other identifiable early survival still clearly visible is the former gate-tower, linked to the present entrance front by a battlemented range.

The keep was extended to the north, or right, of the entrance, possibly in the sixteenth century, to create the present entrance range, and the elevation gained a vague symmetry by the reproduction of a keep-like arrangement further to the right. The whole front was given its present appearance in about 1738 when the 14th Lord Howth, William St Lawrence, modernized some of its interiors. This St Lawrence was a companion of the famous Dean Swift – at least his wife was – and Swift's portrait hangs in the dining room.

Howth retained the main fabric, only regularizing parts of the original. He provided himself with a modern staircase and dining room, simplified access through the building, and probably removed gables from the entrance range to give it a more fashionable, if decidedly squat, effect. The appearance of the seat after this Georgian modernization is recorded in a painting sitting

A view by Henson of Lutyens's new library wing from the parapet of the original keep, showing the distinctive Irish medieval stepping of the battlements and the pyramidal pinnacles, all echoed in Lutyens's tower.

over the drawing-room chimney-piece. In addition to portraying the building it shows the extensive and important, formal classical gardens surrounding the house at that date, remnants of which survive in the modern estate.

Work continued again in the nineteenth century with the involvement of a complex sequence of architects of whom the most significant, in terms of executed work at least, was Richard Morrison. Fortunately the character of the building was adjusted, but not, as happened in so many restorations of that period, destroyed.

Lutyens's great success in his work at Howth is that the house recorded by *Country Life* is recognizably the old, irregular, time-worn fabric it was before he arrived. As the house survives today in much the same form, it remains an important testimony to the care with which the family has continued to tend its ancient seat.

Lutyens's new constructions included the arched loggia (right), *a striking combination of Palladian propriety and provincial pragmatism, and the library* (above), *with elm boarding for the ceiling and oak for the panelling, continuing the Georgian theme.*

Opposite: *Lutyens's landscaping includes the formal parterre along the south front of the east wing, with raised flower beds for better views.*

THREE

CASTLETOWN COX

Co KILKENNY

The appearance of Castletown Cox in *Country Life* in 1918 ushered in the extended if erratic era of the magazine's interest in Irish Georgian architecture. The author is not credited, but the clear style and critical values suggest it is Weaver, and the article is acknowledged as such in his subsequent history of Heywood. Castletown Cox's importance was affirmed by its being the first Irish house to receive the compliment of two articles on its first appearance. It was visited by *Country Life* again in the 1960s when the Knight of Glin presented his study of its architect, Davis Duckart. Situated in the mild southern district of Co. Kilkenny, it has always vied with its Kildare counterpart, Castletown, in both name and history.

Castletown Cox never surpassed its older namesake in scale, quality, associations or variety, yet it has regularly won a special place in the hearts of lovers of Irish architecture. Never suffering the vagaries of neglect, rescue and restoration that dogged the Kildare Castletown, or the radical changes in taste that altered the interior of the older house, Castletown Cox has managed to retain a unique veneer of pristine newness and historical authenticity.

The plan of the house itself is suggestive of these associations. The layout, with a central corridor intersecting the columnar entrance hall, from where it gives access to the rooms extending along its fronts, continues a tradition familiar from the Kildare Castletown. Yet the smaller scale, with only three rooms across its garden front, suggests that such an arrangement, in which so much space is lost to a largely redundant corridor, is more a gratuitous emulation of that earlier house than a functional necessity.

In contrast to Castletown's slow and often mysterious evolution, however, Castletown Cox remains a pure expression of its architect's original intentions, and even its window openings have not been enlarged. Consequently, part of the success of Castletown Cox's original design, and the reason for its survival, must lie in the ease with which the building could accommodate more modern lifestyles inside, with bright interiors of a homely scale, although appearing from the outside as a building parading all the grandeur of the early eighteenth century.

Castletown Cox was built in the early 1770s by Michael Cox, whose surname the house adopts as a suffix to distinguish it from the more famous Castletown. Cox, formerly the Bishop of Ossory, and Archbishop of Cashel from 1755, came from an active family of soldiers and settlers who had made their name and fortune in Ireland since the beginning of the previous century. A younger son, Cox turned towards the Church for his advancement rather than to soldiering or the Bar. This was an area in which he proved himself eminently successful despite – or perhaps because of – his disdain for the politics, pamphleteering and polemics that tended to advance the careers of his fellow clerics. Indeed, his renown was more for his lack of professional interests. One wit attached his own verse to a blank panel, intended for an encomium, on the memorial to the deceased Archbishop:

> Vainest of mortals! Had'st thou sense or grace
> Thou ne'er had'st left this ostentatious space
> Nor given thy numerous foes such ample room
> To tell posterity, upon thy tomb,
> This well-known truth, by every tongue confest,
> That by this blank thy life is well expressed.

Preceding pages: *Castletown Cox, with Henson's view of the entrance that opened its notice in* Country Life.

Left: *The entrance hall as envisaged by Henson in an unpublished view, with the soft furnishings visible in earlier photographs removed to emphasize the architecture. The doorway to the saloon, on the right, with the bust of Archbishop Cox over it, is polite Irish Palladianism at its most mature.*

Despite such a notorious lack of notoriety, by securing the archbishopric of Cashel, Cox gained a position perfectly suitable to his interests, lacking the onerous duties of more famous sees yet with the attraction of a liberal income. This was put to use in building the present house, reputedly assisted by a handsome bequest intended for the construction of a church but redirected towards the Archbishop's own, more worldly interests.

The house-building itself appears to have spanned the years from about 1770 to 1774. The date of completion is confirmed by the rare survival of a bill, submitted by the Irish plasterworker for the house, Patrick Osborne. It details the cost of the different items adorning the interior, from the four capitals in the hall (totalling £11. 7s. 6d.) and the fifty-six festoons in the staircase (at £11s. 4½d. each, coming to a total of £31. 17s.) to the 1,591 feet of

bedroom cornices (totalling £33. 2s. 11d.). The final payment was registered by Osborne's signed receipt dated 19 August 1774 and countersigned by John Nowlan, clerk of works.

Though at Castletown Cox the decorator's work is uncommonly well documented, the identity of the architect is not. Stylistic evidence provided in the *Georgian Society Records*, however, and supported by Weaver and later studies, suggests, with near certainty, that the design of the house derives from the hand of Italian architect Davis Duckart, perhaps more properly referred to as Daviso D'Arcort, then resident in Ireland for less than a decade. Like so many architects in Ireland in the eighteenth century, Duckart remains a figure only tentatively defined. The evidence of his will confirms Continental links, an association suggested by the curious detailing of his architecture. Despite the overall continuity of his work within the rather staid late Palladian styles of Ireland, it has a vigour indicative less of provincial idiosyncrasies than of a personal taste, even if one so outmoded as to be almost returning to fashion at the time.

The house is laid out on Duckart's preferred Palladian tripartite arrangement, with straight arcaded links connecting the residential

Above: The geometric pattern of the saloon ceiling was probably inspired by Irish developments in the Adam style. This design was adapted for another house associated with the same designers, Temple Hill, Blackrock, Co. Dublin.

Right: More lively rococo details appear in the enfilade from the drawing room, through the saloon, to the dining room.

block to flanking pavilions. This gives the building a rather impressive swagger despite the homely scale, for it has only seven bays compared to the Kildare Castletown's thirteen. The broad mass is enlivened by the curves of the pavilion domes and the quirky rustication of the basement. Throughout Duckart's limited body of known and attributed work may be found a similar combination of traditional arrangement and personal detail, but only at Castletown Cox is it so prevalent. Perhaps most surprising is the degree to which Duckart developed his designs for Castletown Cox from traditional sources. As the Knight of Glin observed in his study of Duckart published in *Country Life* in 1967, the main elevations of the house were based on Buckingham House in London, fashionable in the early 1700s.

After enduring a seesaw of ownership that typified so many Irish estates in the nineteenth century, the house was purchased in 1909 by W. H. Wyndham-Quin, later to succeed to the Dunraven

title as the 5th Earl, from Colonel H. J. R. Villiers-Stuart, who had inherited the property. The gardens were the Wyndham-Quins' most important addition to the character of the Georgian house, for they made very few alterations to the building. They produced box hedges and terraces in a rather formulaic sequence, arranged around a series of statues brought over from Clearwell Court, Gloucestershire, but with little of the subtlety of the compartmental gardens then being developed elsewhere in Ireland by Lutyens. The fashion was adopted here also by Norah Lindsay, the Irish-born garden designer, who was a cousin of Wyndham-Quin's wife. It may be that this connection inspired the selection of the house by Weaver, though its full report in the *Georgian Society Records* would also have attracted his attention.

By the time Castletown Cox was featured in the pages of *Country Life*, most of the original furnishings had been dispersed. Weaver considered that the bust of Cox over the door to the saloon might be by Scheemaker, as he had been responsible for the tomb of the Archbishop's second wife. He was complimentary about the modern refurnishing by the new owners, describing it as 'fitting' and showing 'just taste', but he was no less exacting than his photographer in the removal of furniture detrimental to the rigours of the architecture, a point emphasized by comparison with the

photographs of the *Georgian Society Records* which document the more homely character of the rooms in 1913.

Country Life's photographs of Castletown Cox, taken by Henson on a visit in 1917, record the house some eight years after its purchase by the Wyndham-Quins. His presentation of the rooms captures well the variety of Osborne's decorative effects. Stony formality reigns in the hall and staircase hall, with heavy festoons framed by equally heavy moulded panels occasionally tweaked into life by scrolled heads.

Such civility is offset, but never dimmed, by the lively Irish rococo plasterwork of the ceilings. In the rooms at the garden front a lighter air is manifest, and a more progressive style begins to appear. In the original arrangement, as suggested by Osborne's surviving bill, the central saloon would probably have been papered – Weaver considered the possibility of Chinese-style paper found in other interiors of the date – framing the lively and light bracketed cornice and geometrically ordered ceiling. Such plasterwork is much more in the style of Adam, a fashion then promulgated in Ireland by Michael Stapleton. It is a striking contrast with the other ceilings and suggests that Osborne was either learning the newer style or moving between old and new as required by his patron. Certainly this lighter mood provided an effect quite different from that of the two halls, and one that persists in the flanking dining and drawing rooms.

The house was sold by the family in about 1928, two years after Wyndham-Quin had succeeded to the Dunraven title and moved to his family seat, Adare Manor in Co. Limerick. It was purchased by Major-General E. R. Blacque, and sold by his son in 1976 when, with an uncertain future in an unfashionable climate, its survival was secured by the late Brian de Breffny. Given the growing awareness of the importance of the house – it is currently undergoing restoration – together with its manageable scale, its future should never again be in doubt.

Left: *The flanking ranges to the garden have robust arcades. Duckart eschews architectural detail in favour of a broad banding of linked circles – a favourite motif throughout his career.*

Below: *The garden terraces, seen here in an unpublished view, include box hedges and parterres, and were developed by the new owners to add 'incident' to the setting of the house soon after its purchase in about 1909.*

FOUR

HEYWOOD

Co LAOIS

The photographs of Heywood are among the most important results of *Country Life*'s first forays into Ireland.
The destruction of the house by fire in 1950, followed by its demolition, gives these images a unique historic importance. Following a
passing notice in the *Georgian Society Records* of 1913, and a selective, mostly genealogical illustrated history in Sadleir and Dickinson's
Georgian Mansions of 1915, these views, taken by Henson in 1917, are the only serious records of the interiors.
As with Lambay and Howth, this little-known representative of Irish architecture was featured in *Country Life* because
of new work by Edwin Lutyens.

Lutyens's involvement with the garden, alongside the survival of some Adam-style interiors, attracted the attentions of Weaver. He would have been familiar already with the short notices on the house in Irish publications, though in themselves these would not have encouraged him. Lacking either the sophistication of great architecture or the interest of antiquity, the house had little appeal for him. Yet he did recognize the special interest of the building, and it was only the second Irish house to be reviewed by *Country Life* in two separate articles. Henson's photographs also provide a superb record of the early maturity of one of the most striking garden and landscape compositions associated with Lutyens.

Heywood was built by Michael Frederick Trench, cousin to William, 1st Earl of Clancarty, in the early 1770s. The work was reputedly carried out after his own designs, in the manner of the aristocratic designer which was so popular in the eighteenth century. It is probable that he had significant professional assistance, possibly from Richard Johnston, with whom he would be involved over the developments in Dublin, or, perhaps, James Gandon. Photographs show Trench's original building to have been a three-storey, four-bay house with a hipped roof, all features typical of the period.

In the late nineteenth century the original house was encased on the front and sides by a late Victorian mansard-roofed and dormered box of mixed architectural character, none of which enhanced its appeal to Weaver. He described the entrance front as having been 'rebuilt lately' – the *porte-cochère* is dated 1898 – and this may well explain the decision not to publish photographs of this part of the building.

The designs of the original house were noted less for their sophistication than for their comfort. This was reiterated by Weaver, quoting an early description of its 'great family accommodation under moderate external appearance'. Weaver's own comments on the building remain an important critical statement on its internal character: 'The interiors reveal [Trench] as a man of sound taste, but it is true without being malicious to

Preceding pages: *The fountain garden and an unpublished photograph of the garden front as viewed across Trench's original landscaping. The Georgian house, inside its Victorian extension, is signalled by the hipped roof over the central four bays.*

These pages: *Two more unpublished views of Heywood by Henson at his most picturesque: the rear of the now demolished house (above) and the side (right), with Lutyens's surviving pergola viewed from below; the battered and buttressed rampart walls are just visible behind the trees. Trench's landscaping was of limited interest to Weaver.*

say that it is external architecture which finds out the amateur'. If the photographs, published and unpublished, do not wholly confirm this judgement, they do suggest the variable qualities of the interior spaces.

The only interior illustrated fully by Weaver was the dining room, distinguished by its Adam-style work, reminiscent of the neoclassical style of the Irish plasterworker Michael Stapleton. Its walls and ceiling carried Adam-esque motifs in late eighteenth-century geometric style. Though Weaver was not impressed – indeed he used it as a peg to condemn the absence of Irish political autonomy – Sadleir and Dickinson in their *Georgian Mansions* describe it as 'a singularly handsome apartment, and one of the finest examples of the Adam style in this country'. A later author also associated with *Country Life*, Mark Bence-Jones, was to call it 'one of the most accomplished interiors of the Adam period in Ireland'. Beyond these few photographs, there is little else from which we can determine the interior arrangement of the house.

The house itself was situated on what Sadleir and Dickinson described as 'a pretty and tastefully laid out estate', which would have provided a handsome informal foil to the original classical residence. The estate is located near the border with Co. Kilkenny, to the south of Ireland's Midlands, but it is distinguished by an unusually picturesque character distinctively its own, enhanced by Trench's careful layout.

Trench created three artificial lakes, and sited follies and other evocative features in the estate. He also incorporated in his landscape rearranged remnants of the medieval Dominican friary at Aghaboe, and a sixteenth-century tomb, generating an additional *frisson* in the picturesque settings. The intention was for visitors to wend their way along a meandering drive, full of rustic moments and mysterious ruins, to discover the more gentle Claudian landscape, with classical temples carefully disposed, all of which could be viewed best from inside the house.

For Weaver the gardens at Heywood, notably Lutyens's, were its most important feature. Now that the house has been lost and the gardens saved, one might regret the predominance of the garden in these articles, but there is much to support Weaver's case, for they remain one of the finest examples of their art in the country.

Lutyens worked on the gardens from about 1906. He comple-mented the strong architectural framework with an informal planting style, following the same combination of structure and nature developed at Lambay and made popular with his associate – and *Country Life* author – Gertrude Jekyll. Laying out the garden in a series of terraces and stepped passageways exploding east and west from the falling southern terraces of the house itself, the architect shaped these spaces with a bewildering variety of retaining walls – vertical and battered, stepped and sheer – screen walls –

This view of the Georgian drawing room, replete with contemporary and later furnishings, was not published. Unfortunately, the original fireplace was not accorded a separate photograph.

straight and curved, large and dwarf – columns, steps and architectural artefacts.

Lutyens was not especially impressed by his patron, Sir Hutcheson Poë. Weaver remarked on his 'discerning taste as a collector', but Lutyens was struck more by his wooden leg and how 'he sits on a chair and watches the men lay stones – stone by stone – and finds endless fault'; 'I couldn't stand it', he concludes.

The sequence of central terraces, flanked by the pergola to the west and the walled garden to the east, was an almost formal contrast to the more romantic landscaping created by Trench. But much linked the approaches of the two. Lutyens used milestones and stolen capitals in his re-formation of the terracing, a procedure which echoed the Trenches' own relocation of ancient abbey fabric. Yet Weaver criticized Trench rather sharply for his attempt to bring romance to the garden; he described Trench's procedure as

Left: The wall of the pleached alley links house and fountain garden along an area studded with limes and elms, maintaining the architectural theme with oval niches carrying lead busts.

Above: The pergola is another impressive set piece by Lutyens. Breaking forward over the falling land, it gives one of the most dramatic views of the surrounding estate.

'less meritorious' than that followed by Lutyens. Indeed, *Country Life* did not publish any view of the earlier ornaments in the estate's gardens.

A ground plan, published with Weaver's original article, helped clarify the complex relationship between the house and garden – a key element in evaluating Lutyens's response to the commission. For Weaver one of the great successes of Lutyens's garden was its contribution to the architecture of the house. The house, as an amateur production, 'needed … a feeling of strength and support, and a frame of simple yet conscious architectural grace' and these, he goes on to say, are the qualities that Lutyens's work has brought to it. Nowadays, in the absence of the house, it is impossible to evaluate the success of the gardens in these terms. It is evident, however, that they remain significantly impressive on their own, despite the loss of the building.

The estate passed by inheritance to the Poë family, but the house was burned and demolished in 1950. Today the place is owned by the Salesians and serves as a missionary college. New buildings have arisen on the site of the old house, but some of its joinery has been incorporated in the newer work. The future of the gardens has been secured by the state.

FIVE

CASTLETOWN

Co KILDARE

Castletown is Ireland's most important house. In scale, design, execution and, originally, in furnishings, it represented the highest aspirations and first triumph of Ireland's post-medieval culture. Its two major notices in *Country Life*, spanning five articles and thirty-three years, are a part of its more recent history. The articles, by Christopher Hussey in 1936, and Maurice Craig, the Knight of Glin and John Cornforth in 1969 – soon after its rescue by Desmond Guinness and the Irish Georgian Society – together present some of the most memorable scholarship in Irish architectural history.

The association of Castletown with a series of figures seminal both in the evolution of Irish Georgian architecture and in its history, assures it a unique position in Ireland's cultural traditions. Its patron, William Conolly, Speaker to the Irish House of Commons, was energetic in the promotion of the Irish cause, and unbounded in his ambitions for the nation. Consequently the new house he was to build for himself near Celbridge, Co. Kildare, less than fifteen miles from the capital, was conceived on a scale and quality of international stature.

Conolly had made his fortune as one of the shrewdest dealers in an age when, given the impact of the recent wars and penal legislation, land changed hands frequently. He was also one of the most persistent Irish supporters of the royal Hanoverian interests, perhaps perceiving the degree to which the light hand of royalty, represented by George I, would allow political control by Parliament. His own success in Parliament and his political acuity – a perfect match to his financial acumen – gained for him unanimous support in his election, in 1715, as Speaker.

In 1709 Conolly bought the lands of Castletown for £15,000, but first took as his country seat Rodanstown, near Kilcock, before beginning Castletown in about 1719. Soon after this, the celebrated ecclesiastic and philosopher Bishop Berkeley, giving voice to the healthy competition between the resources of the Irish ascendancy and their English counterparts, described the house as being built 'of fine wrought stone, harder and better coloured than the [English] Portland' stone. This fine, light stone was used in the

Preceding pages: Views of Castletown from the Conolly folly, photographed by Gibson, and the lake and the forecourt, by Henson.

Henson's views of the entrance hall (left) and, unpublished, the staircase hall (above left), date to about 1935, when they still retained the family's furniture. Gibson's view of the hall's gallery, taken in about 1969 (above right), shows well the curious basket-headed order in the upper level, with square tapering shafts of Michelangelesque character.

centre block, with a more economical and darker limestone in the advancing wings. Berkeley was also responsible for the tradition that the basement of the house was constructed before the design of the superstructure was decided on and, while there may be some truth in this, recent studies by David Griffin of the Irish Architectural Archive suggest that the plan of the main floor largely corresponds to that of the basement.

Although the detailed history of the design of Conolly's new house remains unconfirmed, it seems almost certain that the Speaker – as he was popularly known – employed an Italian architect, Alessandro Galilei, to generate the main design. That he should look to a Continental designer suggests the international context in which he and his friends envisaged the future development of Ireland. That the work on the house should be completed by Edward Lovett Pearce, an Irish architect of equal ability, if rather less renown, also indicates the confidence that Conolly was prepared to show in native talent.

Galilei, back in Italy by the time building began in 1719, maintained contact with Ireland through Pearce, but soon turned to more immediate concerns in Rome, notably the completion of the Basilica San Giovanni in Laterano. He left behind in Ireland a taste of the Italian city palazzo represented by the elevation of Castletown's central block. In contrast, Pearce's importance in Irish Georgian architecture lay in his responsibility for introducing

the fashionable neo-Palladian style into the country, a manner then under development in England by figures such as Lord Burlington. At Castletown, his first major work, he overlaid this more delicate manner on to Galilei's robust fabric, creating a highly individual building.

Pearce's role appears to have been limited to the internal arrangements and the pavilions. His most notable surviving interior is the two-storey entrance hall, panelled and articulated with screens of columns to the rear. The curious detailing of the columns on the upper floor is reminiscent of the baroque manner, a remnant of his training under one of the great masters in the English baroque, Sir John Vanbrugh. Vanbrugh, it should be remembered, was also related to Pearce; this perhaps furthered his influence on the younger man.

The complex history of the building of the house, and the paucity of documentation, renders it almost impossible to establish entirely the different hands involved. Distinguishing between the Anglicized Italian, Galilei, and the Irish Italophile, Pearce, is difficult enough, but the story is convoluted further by the involvement of lesser personalities. Details of their known contemporary work – in the case of Thomas Burgh, the next most significant name, the distinctly old-fashioned Dr Steeven's Hospital in Dublin – do little to support a significant stylistic association with Conolly's house and its comparatively sophisticated detailing.

Castletown evolved with the changing tastes of its residents, and throughout the century the Conolly family continued to bring to the house the variety of fashionable interests and political ideas developing in Georgian Ireland. After the death of the childless Speaker and his wife, the house eventually devolved to his great-nephew, Tom Conolly. He and his wife Lady Louisa, daughter of the 2nd Duke of Richmond and sister to Emily, Duchess of Leinster, brought a new vitality to the house on taking up residence there in 1758. Complementing Tom's self-conscious Irish patriotism, which ensured that Castletown would remain at the centre of Irish politics to the end of the century, Lady Louisa brought a sense of taste and fashion that reshaped the character of the original house into a form easily recognizable today.

Indeed, actual construction work continued into the second half of the century, notably with the completion of the staircase hall. Designed by Simon Vierpyl to fit into the still unfinished space of the original building, this broad and bright construction carries a brass balustrade signed and dated 'A. King, Dublin, 1760'. The room is further enriched by plasterwork executed by the famous Lafranchini family of stuccodores. The devotion of such a large

The long gallery, before the loss of its contents, contained an exceptional and eclectic collection, unfortunately not reported on separately by Country Life. *The central door-and-niche arrangement dates to the remodelling of the interior from the 1770s. The lunette linking the doors is after Guido Reni's* Aurora, *and the statue of Diana between reputedly 'smuggled out of Greece in a coffin'. In front of these, the Broadwood pianoforte, dated 1790, belonged to Lady Louisa Conolly. The chandeliers are Venetian.*

internal space to circulation harks back to the early eighteenth-century origins of the house. So too does the plasterwork, which recalls an age far removed from the delicacies of neoclassical taste which were soon to reform interiors here, as in so many other Irish houses.

The neoclassical revolution transformed Castletown's most distinctive interior, the long gallery on the first floor. This type of room, with its inordinately long proportions, is of pre-Renaissance derivation, and may even have been included in the designs at the instigation of the Speaker himself. The magnificent compartmented ceiling, restored in recent years, is by Pearce, but many of the other details are part of the extensive redecoration and remodelling undertaken under the immediate direction of Lady Louisa. Most surprising is the Pompeiian arabesque decoration of the walls, executed in 1775–6 by Charles Ruben Riley and Thomas Ryder. Many of the devices were adapted from prints from Renaissance sources, such as Raphael's decoration of the Vatican Loggia. The dining room and drawing rooms were also altered, while the print room, by 1936 the billiard room, was given its titular ornaments by Lady Louisa herself in about 1770.

Castletown continued to exemplify many aspects of Irish cultural awareness in its later history. In this century it has been central to a growing understanding of the importance of Irish historic architecture. Having featured as the centrepiece of the *Georgian Society Records*' volume on Irish country houses in 1913, in 1965 the estate was sold for development, marking the nadir of one of the most threatening periods for Irish architectural heritage. In 1967, with the house empty and already suffering vandalism, it was purchased by Desmond Guinness, and served as the headquarters for the Irish Georgian Society. In more recent years, after heroic efforts by the Society to maintain the fabric and develop the house as a resource, Castletown has been taken into state care, in final if belated recognition of its historic and cultural importance.

Left: *Hussey admired the library 'for its unusually complete mahogany furnishing in a late Adam style … surrounded by bookshelves … in which a draw-out flap is provided … [while] chairs, side and centre tables – the latter intended as a double writing table – are en suite'.*

Above: *The dining room, viewed here in about 1935, was attributed first to Pearce, then to William Chambers, while more recent research suggests the inspiration of a less well-known English architect, Isaac Ware.*

SIX

CARTON

Co KILDARE

The house at Carton, an estate originally owned by the FitzGeralds, Earls of Kildare, was theirs for a comparatively short part
of the family's expansive history. Their Irish roots originated with the Norman invasion, when Maurice FitzGerald was granted lands and
lordship in recognition of his services, but Carton established itself as their seat only after its remodelling from 1739 for Robert FitzGerald,
19th Earl. The earlier house was recorded in a painting as a building in what has been called a Dutch Palladian style. Although the
old Carton was more a modern seat than a castle, it still lacked that fashionable mien expected of one of the greatest families in Ireland.
Consequently Richard Castle, the most successful architect then in the country, was called in to upgrade the existing building.

The exact scope of Castle's new work – and how much was left of the older structure – remains unclear. Certainly the confusion of layouts and levels in the present building, even allowing for the extent of later alterations, suggests that Castle did not have complete freedom in his plans. However, he did regularize and extend the house, and he refaced it and added new carved heraldry in the pediment, made by local Irish masons John Haughton and John Kelly. Further alterations in the nineteenth century resulted in the loss of what must have been one of the more impressive features – the staircase – but Castle's saloon remains among the most grandiose domestic interiors in the country.

Rising from walls enriched in part with Victorian decoration – including an organ designed by Lord Gerald FitzGerald and inserted in 1857 – the steep and populous cove terminates in a sparse compartmented flat occupied by Jupiter. With its cavorting gods, the design follows a tradition of richly modelled figurative ceilings in a baroque style still popular – if seldom affordable – in mid-Georgian Ireland. The scheme itself is a typically allusive classical arrangement of lordly couples, following a theme that has been summarized most simply as 'The Courtship of the Gods'. It was composed and executed by a family of plasterworkers traditionally referred to, almost generically, as the 'Italian Francini', and more recently identified as the Swiss Lafranchini. The organ, barely shown in *Country Life*'s photographs, perhaps because of its Victorian origins, follows the style of its setting.

The other significant mid-eighteenth-century interior was the so-called Chinese bedroom, the decoration of which postdates Castle's involvement with the building. He had died at Carton in 1751, reportedly while writing a letter concerning work at the family's Dublin town house, then under construction. The bedroom itself is an important Irish example of the taste for things Chinese so prevalent then, and this work may be associated with the 20th Earl, James, and his wife.

James succeeded to the title in 1744 and three years later married the famous Lady Emily Lennox, daughter of the 2nd Duke of Richmond and sister to Louisa, who would eventually take up residence at nearby Castletown. The 20th Earl, later the 1st Duke of Leinster, and his wife found a house largely complete, and concerned themselves mostly with the development of the landscape. They tried to attract Lancelot 'Capability' Brown but failed. It is said that he thanked them for their offer of £1,000 to come to Ireland, but considered himself too busy finishing England. So they re-formed the estate themselves, creating one of the most important Georgian landscapes in the country. This gave

Preceding pages: *The exterior, from the garden, alongside an unpublished view of the saloon, dramatically swept of furniture, photographed by Henson in August 1935.*

Right: *Richard Castle created a typical early Georgian ashlar box linked to wings by curved colonnades. Remodelling by Richard Morrison replaced the latter with the straight links of coupled columns seen in this previously unpublished view.*

to the house an almost idyllic setting, as they planted clumps of trees and blocked the adjacent Rye river to form a serpentine lake.

The effect was enhanced by the next generation. The 2nd Duke, being particularly interested in farming developments, increased the estate to sixty thousand acres and enclosed some eleven hundred inside a five-mile wall that still survives.

The integration of soft and varied landscape, gently spotted with architecture such as the bridge designed by the Irish contemporary of James Gandon, Thomas Ivory, was exactly the effect Capability Brown would have sought. The survival of this landscape today, largely unaltered and within the original walled demesne, marks this estate as one of the most significant of its type.

Although the 2nd Duke appears to have consulted James Wyatt about altering and extending the house, it was the 3rd Duke who,

Left: The dining room was Richard Morrison's most important interior at Carton, though he was also responsible for the plainer staircase. The robust plasterwork seen here was executed by Christopher Moore.

Below: The Chinese bedroom, in which Queen Victoria slept, was decorated in 1759. The taste of the Oriental is pervasive, even to the plasterwork. The chimney-piece, however, is later.

shortly after attaining his majority in 1812, initiated the next major phase of work. The new Duke considered the family's Dublin residence, Leinster House – today's Parliament house or Dáil – surplus to their needs: with the demise of the Irish Parliament at the turn of the century, there was little point in maintaining an expensive house in the capital. It was decided to sell this and improve their main country seat.

The historian Brian FitzGerald, in *Country Life,* identified the Duke himself as the author of the alterations, with the Irish neoclassical architect Richard Morrison acting as executor. More recent research has drawn attention also to the importance of the role possibly played by Francis Johnston, architect of Townley Hall, Co. Louth, in these first phases of extension.

It may have been Johnston who designed the first radical rearrangement of the house, as drawings relating to his office suggest, perhaps even reordering some of the main interiors. He may have taken a hand in turning Castle's original entrance front, with its flanking pavilions, into the present garden front, and was perhaps responsible for the Doric porch on the new garden front, since it appears as existing fabric on plans for alterations prepared

in Morrison's office. If this porch is by Johnston, then Morrison's remodelling owes much to him. Morrison picked up the Doric motif and intertwined it through end windows and new colonnades in order to tie the expansive design together.

Inside, Morrison had more freedom to develop new rooms behind his colonnades. Most notable was the dining room, situated behind the columns on the right of the garden front. Here he developed one of his most striking interiors, using columnar screens at either end of a segmental-vaulted rectangular room. Its rich plasterwork, executed by Christopher Moore, was a remarkable anticipation of the style of the Morrisons' family practice in the 1820s, so well represented at Ballyfin, Co. Laois. The Duke also managed to incorporate a chimney-piece from his former Dublin house, distinguished by its four shafts of yellow Siena marble, in the new dining room.

The judicious consolidation of the family's finances in the nineteenth century did not secure the future of Carton in the next. The 7th Duke, who succeeded to the title unexpectedly after the death of his elder brother, had already signed away his inheritance to Sir Henry Mallaby-Deeley in return for guaranteed capital and an annuity, and since 1949 the house has passed through a number of hands. Its fabric has survived well even if many of the contents have not, but unfortunately it is at present, together with its magnificent estate, under threat of development.

Above: *A marble boy by Quellin, the Flemish sculptor, dated 1696.*

Right: *The eastern end of the long lawn in front of the house. The 'undulating and well-timbered estate of 1,200 acres ... through [which] the artificial river known as the Ryewater winds its way' was not recorded further by Country Life.*

SEVEN

RUSSBOROUGH

Co WICKLOW

When in 1937 Brian FitzGerald expressed his satisfaction at the rescue of Russborough from an uncertain future, he voiced a general concern for the situation of Ireland's Georgian heritage. He could not have known the hazardous times that lay ahead for such houses, but he would nevertheless have appreciated the sense of relief in 1951 when the house, again for sale in an insecure market, was purchased by Sir Alfred Beit Bt, one of the great art collectors of his day, for use as his home and as a setting for his world-famous art collection. Russborough is located near Blessington, Co. Wicklow, about twenty miles south-west of Dublin. The estate is not especially far from Powerscourt, in the same county, and shares with it not only the architect, Richard Castle, an extensive elevation, and the remnants of an original formal garden – at Powerscourt overlaid in the nineteenth century – but also the manner of approaching the house.

The visitor to each comes to the house from the side, an arrangement not uncommon in the grander Irish house, and possibly inspired by Castletown or Carton. Despite these similarities with a more majestic tradition in Irish Georgian country houses, however, Russborough encapsulates a rather different, and in many ways a more gentle and informal mood.

Over the seven hundred feet of its extent only seven bays are given to the house proper, which is itself quite small. Yet this must reflect the needs and aspirations of the man who built it, Joseph Leeson, an enthusiastic collector, Italophile and developer who eventually gained for himself the prestigious title of 1st Earl of Milltown. Leeson, as he then was, inherited his fortune in 1741 from his father, a successful Dublin brewer, and in the same year purchased from John Graydon the lands later transformed into the Russborough estate. He immediately set about developing the demesne with the same enthusiasm shown by so many of his contemporaries for the newly popular Italian and Palladian traditions. Even so, he displayed more taste than some, and a more acute sense of the limitations of his own finances than most.

Leeson's development of the garden terraces was extravagant. The house gained its fine prominence from sitting on an embankment created by the opening of the lakes and ponds, all reputedly costing some £30,000. Despite appearances, the residential part of the house adopted a more homely scale, extending only three rooms across. More importantly, it was provided with a lavish and consistent decoration throughout its

Preceding pages: *A view along the approach taken by Gibson in about 1963, and across the lower lake by Henson in about 1935.*

These pages: *More views by Gibson, showing* (left) *the front after the reinstatement of the windows by Lord Beit; Cornforth still considered the elevation too flat compared to the colonnades. The lions carry the heraldic shield of the Milltowns. The full front* (above), *which stretches to some seven hundred feet including kitchen and stable wings and farmyards, in a view almost exactly repeating one by Henson.*

main interiors. As the very smallness of Russborough assisted in its completion in a generally uniform style, so too that smallness has helped it survive less polite centuries than the eighteenth, when it could offer the necessary practical comforts that larger Georgian houses failed to do.

Leeson not only succeeded in securing Ireland's most successful architect, and probably then its busiest, for the design of the new house, but he also secured from him a design that, though not without its faults, might be listed among Castle's more thoughtful. Its front is faced in dressed granite from the nearby Golden Hill quarry, and the different functions of the building's elements are appropriately distinguished through Castle's frank, if unsubtle,

Left: The new dining room after Captain Daly had temporarily reinstated part of Milltown's original scheme by replacing the George Barret landscapes in their frames. The chimney-piece first inspired the young Alfred Beit's interest in the house, and he copied its design for his London home.

Above: The saloon in about 1935, superbly preserved with its original crimson cut velvet over the heavy dado panelling, mahogany doors, marble chimney-piece and fine parquet floor with a satinwood star. The ceiling putti suggest the Lafranchini.

use of the orders: Corinthian for the residence, Doric for the colonnades, Ionic for the advancing wings, and a robust astylar treatment for the ranges beyond.

As with so many Irish houses, the detailed history of the building is largely conjectural, developing around a series of disconnected dates. Of these the most important, after 1741 which saw the actual purchase of the land, are 1743 when Leeson was elected MP, 1748 when Russborough was described as a 'noble new house forming into perfection', and 1752 when Bishop Pococke called it 'a new built house'. Its progress was punctuated by Leeson's visits to Rome, in 1744 and 1751, both of which involved extensive purchases of Roman material. His latter visit took place in the year that Castle died, at Carton. As the growing collection continued to shape the house a second architect must have been involved, and responsibility for work on the fabric after Castle's death has generally been attributed to Francis Bindon, a successful artist and architect in mid-Georgian Ireland. We may see his hand in the bedrooms, where at last the rigorous rectilinear geometry of the walls finally eases, and curved corners begin to make an appearance.

Outside, the house suggests little of the extravagance apparent inside, a feature that Brian FitzGerald, writing about the house for *Country Life*, observed as being typical of Irish Georgian architecture. For John Cornforth, author of *Country Life*'s second series on the house, no less typically Irish was its combination of Palladian propriety and the 'unaffected air that takes away any feeling of bombast that there could be in such an extensive design'.

Inside, there is a remarkable combination of formal disposition of spaces and free expression in decoration, traditional in Irish architecture. The entrance hall provides the visitor with the first sense of happy disorientation, for after the austerity of the exterior, run through with a tasteful and economical thread of classical rigour, the elaborate plasterwork and rich furnishings provide a surprisingly successful counterpoint. The compartmented ceiling also gives an initial impression of architectural formality, though a closer study provides a real anticipation of the details to come.

Determining authorship of the plasterwork is still somewhat controversial, and the clear evidence of different hands suggests that there is no simple answer. Certainly the Lafranchini family, who worked at Carton and Castletown, may be cited, but the greatest surprise here is the unmitigated extravagance of the

stucco in the staircase hall. This must surely suggest the hand of a less restrained artist, presumably local. The timber staircase itself is finished with exemplary care, using Tuscan columns reminiscent of Castletown, Co. Kildare, but also taking the opportunity to add a few extra meandering curves to its alignment at the head of the stairs.

Leeson's visits to Rome, supported by his private wealth and public positions, allowed him to amass one of the finest art collections of its day in the country. He did all that was expected of the gentleman on tour to Italy, mixing with the cultured English-speaking visitors to Rome, enjoying their less formal lifestyle, having his portrait painted by Batoni, and buying innumerable works of art. His own purchases during the visits were supplemented by a network of dealers acting for him, including the Irishman Robert Wood, presumably the same Wood better known for his travels to Palmyra and Baalbek.

The entrance hall in about 1935 (below), *with an unpublished view* (right). *The cut-glass chandelier, which had hung in the British Embassy in Paris, complements the vigorous modelling of wall, ceiling, doorcases and chimney-piece. The neoclassical chairs flanking the pedimented door came from Dunsandle, Co. Galway, and may be compared to similar pieces at Castlecoole.*

Wood's name is also associated with one of the happiest moments in the recent history of the house. In 1749 he ordered for Leeson four oval paintings from the talented Italian artist Vernet, and these were hung in specially designed frames in the drawing room. Some time before the house was bought by Captain Denis Daly of Dunsandle, Co. Galway, in 1931, but after its appearance in the *Georgian Society Records* in 1913, the paintings were removed. In Henson's photographs of the room in the mid-1930s, and in Gibson's of the early 1960s, their vacant frames stare out like gouged sockets. It was not until the 1970s that the Vernets were tracked down by Lord Beit, who took the rare opportunity to reinstate an Irish interior.

Although the 1st Earl's hanging arrangements have been lost, Ireland may still count itself remarkably fortunate. In 1902, the

Left: FitzGerald described the exotically energetic plasterwork of the staircase hall as 'a riot of rococo', perhaps still failing to convey its unique power.

Above: The top-lit lobby on the first floor gives access to the bedrooms, and is a popular arrangement in Georgian Ireland. Henson's photograph shows it before its remodelling by Lord Beit. The Tuscan columns of the staircase, in the distance, are reminiscent of those at Castletown.

widow of the 7th and last Earl bequeathed the collection to the National Gallery of Ireland, creating the famed Milltown bequest. After that happy event, the house stood dangerously idle for some years until Captain Daly purchased it in 1931 and commenced restoration, in addition to filling it with some of his own art collection. It is this period of the complex history of the house that Henson records in his generous photographs.

The most recent phase, marked by the purchase of Russborough by Sir Alfred Beit in 1951, introduced a whole new dimension to the house as a home for fine art; his collection includes works by important artists such as Rembrandt and Vermeer. As John Cornforth has astutely observed, Beit's remarkable collection is untypical of the Irish country house tradition. This is because it lacks the more ordinary works, ambitiously ascribed to greater hands, that the typical country house collection amasses over the many years of its life. Yet perhaps this makes Russborough all the more appropriate as the modern home for these works, for it is itself an untypical jewel, being so successful a representation of a single period in Irish architecture, and itself surviving so wonderfully well.

EIGHT

CASTLECOOLE

Co FERMANAGH

Castlecoole was under development from about 1788 as the new residence for the 1st Lord Belmore, created Viscount in 1789, and, in 1797, 1st Earl of Belmore. Intended to replace the attractive if old-fashioned existing house – which burned down in 1797 – the new home established its credentials through impeccable taste and workmanship. It was these qualities that secured its recognition as one of Ireland's greatest country houses although, costing some £54,000, it left the family deeply in debt on the death of the Earl. The house is situated in Ulster's Co. Fermanagh, on the rich land lying between the upper and lower lakes of Lough Erne, and alongside the meandering River Erne that connects them.

The elegant park takes its name from the ancient barony of Coole, and shares it with the adjacent Lough Coole. This lake retains Ireland's only breeding colony of greylag geese, introduced in about 1700 by the Corry family, who first developed the estate, and whose descendants, as Lords Belmore, built the present house. The geese have a special place in the family's history, as it is said that should they ever leave, so too would the Belmores.

Castlecoole was largely designed by James Wyatt, who in his earlier years had matched the brothers Adam with his own brand of classical eclecticism, as represented by his interiors at Curraghmore, Co. Waterford. He later gained further regard for his abilities in handling the increasingly popular Gothic style. Indeed, Wyatt's taste swung in perfect time with fashionable taste, and at Castlecoole he showed total control of the peculiar brand of progressive mainstream classicism, regardless of particular historical style, that he had for long made his own.

In the 1790s a style, originating in William Chambers's severe French neoclassical manner, became especially popular. Unhampered by archaeological pretensions which were to come in the next century, the taste, as represented by Castlecoole, was for taut sharp lines unencumbered by irrelevant architectural detail.

An interest in evoking the austerity of Greek architecture, as opposed to Roman, abounded, but direct copyings were rejected in favour of references and variations. In the colonnades on the entrance front to Castlecoole, for example, Wyatt used the baseless column associated with the most severe Greek styles, although the capitals are more Roman, and seem almost fussy by comparison.

Castlecoole's entrance and garden fronts, photographs of which opened Hussey's article, captured the sharp geometry of Wyatt's original design, with the crisp lines of the drawings reinterpreted in the superbly cut Portland stone of these ashlar fronts. The scale is suitably majestic, with freestanding columns on the entrance front – each consisting of 'six drums averaging 4ft. 6ins. high' – rising

Preceding pages: Henson's views of the entrance front, taken in about 1935. Hussey criticized the 'lack of incident', suggesting that this might be 'counteracted if the window framing were painted white instead of black'.

Below: The dining room, with the light relief of ceiling and chimney-piece, trim panels on the wall and delicate furniture, is a perfect example of 1790s taste. The ceiling was executed by the plasterers sent over by Joseph Rose and supervised by a Mr Shires – or Sheirs – at a cost of £63.

Right: The entrance hall, with columnar screen. The discrepancy between the axis of hall and staircase is corrected on the other side of the door.

the full height of the building. The arrangement was intended to recall the single-storey Greek temple, but here it is applied to a two-storey elevation. The pavilions, or wings, betray a more mixed pedigree. Their front elevations are inspired by the ends of the Custom House in Dublin, designed by the greatest architect working in late-eighteenth century Ireland, James Gandon.

Hussey's discussion of Castlecoole displays his ability to transform the records of a building – records often lacking in any obvious contemporary human significance – into a perfect picture of the past. Consider, for example, the selection of extracts he

Left: The effect of the double return of the staircase is somewhat undermined by Wyatt's fudging, with columns on the first floor standing over open space below. His correction of the alignment between the stairs and the door to the hall – using a false door – shows a wittier Wyatt.

Above: The saloon was fitted up in the 1790s, when Joseph Rose's workmen complained bitterly about the facilities provided on site. In the 1800s it gained the monumental furnishings that contrast with the lighter details of the original decoration.

makes from the early reports on the building, using workers' payments and private accounts to draw the reader into the real world of the construction of Castlecoole:

From the weekly returns it is possible to visualise the immense undertaking as it proceeded. First of all, from the Autumn of 1788 till November 1789, the work of levelling the site, in places lowering it as much as 12ft., and excavating the basement was begun. The brig *Martha* was chartered to carry stone from Portland to Ballyshannon, where a quay was specially built. Thence the great blocks were carried on bullock carts across the eight miles to Lough Erne, on which it was shipped to a quay at Enniskillen, more bullock carts bringing it the last two miles to the site. Already in February, 1790, a few stone cutters were at work, and in May there were eight masons. The number soon increased to thirty-five. In June, 1791, when the work was at its height, the wages bill was £159. 13s. 7½d., and there were twenty-five stone-cutters, twenty-six stone-masons, ten stone-sawyers, seventeen carpenters and eighty-three labourers.

Despite his careful research, Hussey did not uncover the role played by an Irish architect in the evolution of the design, Richard

Johnston. Johnston signed the drawings for a closely related – if in detail significantly different – architectural scheme prepared for Lord Belmore. In contrast to what Hussey described as Wyatt's restrained 'Attic simplicity, Doric massiveness', Johnston's design was all pilaster and ornamental trimmings, harking back to an earlier tradition.

Despite the shortage of documentary evidence, the persistence of many of the features from an earlier manner into Wyatt's executed work was sensed by Hussey, though he attributed these to Wyatt's own eclectic tastes. He remarked on the traditional plan, and the 'Palladian' survival of balustraded parapet, Venetian windows – in the rear of the wings – and the pert hipped roof. His attribution of these features to Wyatt's stylistic vagaries is not unreasonable, and may have some basis in fact. The Venetian windows, for example, do not seem to come from Johnston, though they remain the most incongruous elements in the exterior. However, if through lack of information, the source for the occasional old-fashioned detail is misrepresented, the acuity of Hussey's observations, and the sensitivity of his judgements, is well confirmed.

Adapting in his first-floor lobby an internal two-storey arrangement, Wyatt shrewdly provides circulation for a third storey, hidden behind his two-storey elevation outside. Hussey's suggestion that the source of the columns' design is 'the super-imposed columns in the interiors of the Parthenon and the Temple of Poseidon at Paestum' is less inspiring than his observations on this space. He identifies Wyatt's coupling of freestanding columns, and the dramatic contrasts of perspectives, light wells and lanterns, with the architectural drama that gives his Gothic designs such life. He also sees that 'there is even a traceable connection between the dramatic austerity of this composition and the interior of Salisbury Cathedral, stripped, scraped, and lengthened to produce the aesthetic effect known at the time as the sublime'.

The most impressive room remains the saloon, situated directly on an axis with the front door and extruding its curved mass to enliven the garden front. The room was fitted up at the end of the 1790s, when the plasterer Joseph Rose of London sent over workmen to execute Wyatt's designs. Dominic Bartoli worked on the scagliola marbling of the shafts, and the plaster Corinthian capitals came from London.

It has long been evident that much of the house was furnished only in the early years of the nineteenth century, as the heavier lines and sturdier classical details of many of the contents contrast with the lighter taste of Wyatt's and Rose's décor. However, the details of this later work for long remained unclear. In 1986 Gervase Jackson-Stops reported in *Country Life* on the discovery

of the accounts concerning the furnishing of the house, clarifying the history and once again reaffirming the continuing importance of *Country Life* in disseminating current developments in the study of Ireland's architectural history. The documents provided confirmation of a previously tenuous link suggesting the involvement of Dublin upholsterers, John and Nathaniel Preston of Henry Street, and recorded the extent of their involvement in the completion of the decoration. In 1807 the 2nd Earl first called on the firm, and they were responsible eventually for some £26,367 worth of decoration and furnishing in the house, all carried out over the ensuing eighteen years.

Jackson-Stops was able to provide detailed histories of the whole commission. The bow room, situated over the saloon and unrecorded by *Country Life*, was the earliest to be associated with the firm, and its furnishings included twelve satinwood chairs, billed for in 1809, pier tables, two sofas and a bamboo settee. In 1815 the 'Grecian style' sofas in the oval saloon were sent from Dublin, while the furnishing of the state bedroom, completed in 1821, appears to mark the conclusion of the major work.

Since 1951 Castlecoole has been maintained by the National Trust for Northern Ireland, and the interiors, fitted out, furnished and lovingly maintained intact by the family, continue to impress both for their magnificent quality and for the curious, but satisfying, conjunction of tastes from two quite different centuries.

Left: *Although largely designed by an English architect, Castlecoole has many references to Irish traditions, not least this sophisticated variation on the top-lit lobby, connecting with surrounding rooms.*

Right: *The basement kitchen, with the vaulting which supports the super-structure piercing the space, was one of the earliest illustrations in* Country Life *of a service area in an Irish house.*

NINE

CALEDON

Co TYRONE

Like many Irish country houses, Caledon in Co. Tyrone has evolved through the gradual extension and enveloping of earlier fabric; unlike many such houses, however, the starting point for Caledon was not a medieval core, but a late eighteenth-century house. Built from 1779 for a retired trader, the building was encased in early nineteenth-century fabric that continued the smartly sensitive classicism of the original. Its remarkable interiors fully justified its inclusion as the last house in Christopher Hussey's first informal series on Irish houses. The original house at Caledon was designed by a talented contemporary of James Gandon, Thomas Cooley, for James Alexander, newly retired from successful and lucrative service with the East India Company. Alexander returned to Ireland in 1772, evidently intent on enhancing his aristocratic credentials through judicious use of his recently won fortune.

He used his fortune to develop estates to the value of £600,000. Forgoing his recently built Boom Hall in Derry, designed by Michael Priestly, Alexander took advantage of the opportunity to purchase the prestigious Caledon estate, originally Kinaird or Kennard Castle, from the absentee 7th Earl of Orrery.

The existing house, described by Dean Swift as being 'old, low, and, though full of rooms, not very large', was unsuited to the aspirations of the retired 'nabob', as such traders were commonly described. Selecting a new site and a fashionable Dublin architect, he set about the development of his seat. The house was a crisp but sparse two-storey range with a pediment to the front and a bow to the rear – a perfect expression of the restrained neoclassical taste of the later eighteenth century. Cooley also designed the stable block, this time in a fashion recalling William Chambers's earlier stables at Goodwood House, West Sussex.

No less successful than the new house was the development of Alexander's political interests. From gaining his Parliamentary

seat soon after his return to Ireland, he progressed quickly to being created Baron Caledon in 1790, Viscount in 1797, and finally, with the Union and not long before his death in 1802, he received his earldom. It was his son, Dupré, the 2nd Earl, who was responsible for the extension of the house, for which he called in the highly fashionable English architect John Nash. The Earl, a Knight of St Patrick, was also a liberal developer of his estate and he built new cottages, and laid out the town of Caledon, paying £3,000 to provide it with a new courthouse.

Preceding pages: *Nash's Regency colonnade of about 1812 fronts a house originally of two storeys. The* porte-cochère *provided a new entrance in 1835.*

These pages: *Cooley's original entrance hall* (above) *was adapted as a saloon in 1835. The scagliola columns and frieze, though eighteenth century, help the room carry the heavier gilt furniture. Nash's library* (right) *combines dome, square and columns to create a dramatic internal picturesque, superbly captured by Henson.*

Hussey recognized the complex interaction of patron and architect, and his history of the house identified two sources for Nash's most important external work, the colonnade across the entrance front. On the one hand, as a governor of the Cape of Good Hope from 1806 until his return to Caledon in 1811, the 2nd Earl, Hussey observed, would have been aware of the advantages of the 'stoep', or verandah, of the Dutch houses there. He might well have desired a comparable, if classically refined version of the feature at his own seat. Nash interpreted this by turning to more familiar ground, and using a design he adapted from that of the colonnades of his London streetscapes, such as Park Crescent and Old Regent Street.

In itself a happy product of sympathetic minds, the strong projection forward of the colonnade from the original house must have led to the dwarfing of Cooley's two-storey building. Perhaps in recognition of the inordinate dominance of Nash's colonnade, in the final phase of work on Caledon, which began in 1835, again under the 2nd Earl, a third floor was added to the eighteenth-century house. This not only improved proportions, but also provided useful additional space. Associated developments at this time also enhanced the formal reception spaces, as a new *porte-cochère* and entrance hall were built along the east side of the house.

The alterations of 1835 enabled the Earl to transform finally Cooley's original building into the Caledon described by Hussey and recorded by Henson. Indeed it is inside the house that we find

Above: *The modern boudoir has a gently domical ceiling recalling work at Lucan House, Co. Dublin, with painted panels that, on the basis of 'their more masculine style', Hussey attributed to William Hamilton. Elsewhere, patterns included 'chocolate triangles framing pink squares ... tortoiseshell with white'.*

Right: *Cooley's planning also echoed Lucan and other contemporary Irish houses, as in the oval drawing room. The ornament is executed in papier-mâché while the marble chimney-piece, 'cut on the curve to fit the room', appeared to Hussey to be a Continental import.*

the most thrilling of Caledon's delights, and the clear justification for its inclusion in Hussey's selection of Irish houses.

The rooms of the original house combine features of different styles and dates, all in a surprisingly successful manner. The boudoir in particular, with its imported Chinese paper, Adamesque trim to the ceiling and Regency furnishings, finds unity in a colour scheme of apple green and chocolate brown recorded in detail by Hussey in acknowledgement of the limitations of his monochrome magazine.

With the extensions of 1835, the original entrance hall, situated behind Nash's colonnade, could serve as a formal saloon. Overlaid on Cooley's standard arrangement, stoic and Doric, are furnishings of a much more exuberant nineteenth-century taste, puffed up and full of gilded carving. The oval drawing room, with its deep-cut niches so effectively exaggerated in Henson's wide-angled views, successfully combined elements from at least the first two, and perhaps all three periods in the development of the fabric of the house.

Nash's most important new interior is the library, situated behind the apparently blind western pavilion of his extension. It is a tremendous architectural orchestration in which books, impressed into the wall, play a remarkably subordinate role. Indeed its furnishings are dominated by Thomas Lawrence's portraits of George III and Queen Charlotte, painted with his usual flair, and superbly framed, giving to the room an especially exuberant character. The last phase of extensions, attributed to James Pennethorne, successor to Nash's practice, captures effectively an abstract simplicity that, in the new hall in particular, could not fail to impress. At its least effective, however, as in the portico to the *porte-cochère*, it combines a rather dry correctness of detail with an unsatisfactory freedom of composition. Hussey, with his unfailing acuity of taste, acknowledged the consistency of this last work with Nash's own manner and observed that, with these later additions being 'so close a perpetuation of his style', then 'Caledon might well be taken to represent him among the country houses of the British Isles'. Happily, the house remains so today.

Below: *Seen from the terraces, the south front with the central bow of Cooley's building explains well the form of the original house, despite the addition of the top floor and the new entrance arrangement, seen on the right, in about 1835.*

Right: *One of the magnificent groves of Irish yew, which so impressed Hussey. In 1915 the estate was described as 'singularly pretty ... with a well-stocked deer park, some ornamental water, and ... plantations of well-grown trees'.*

POWERSCOURT

Co WICKLOW

Powerscourt holds a special place in the Irish imagination. It possesses both romantic associations, through its picturesque surroundings and history, and a tragic, more recent past in which the interior was gutted by fire in November 1974, just prior to its intended opening to the public. Because of the loss of its historic rooms the records of the building made by *Country Life* in 1946 are of especial importance. The older history of Powerscourt is no less dramatic, as its magnificent Georgian interiors were neatly inserted into a pre-existing structure. It may be surprising that Powerscourt did not feature in Hussey's first selection of houses in the 1930s. Perhaps its reserved notice in the bible of grand Irish country houses, the *Georgian Society Records*, dissuaded him.

Certainly the judgement passed by the book was harsh, dismissing the house as 'Remodelled rather than built', and granting it only one photograph. To this day this masterpiece, attributed to that most prolific of Irish Georgian architects Richard Castle, remains undervalued in Ireland's architectural history.

The house was developed on an estate in Wicklow that, through its mountainous terrain and its proximity to the Anglo-Norman capital of Dublin, proved most treacherous to the stability of medieval and Renaissance Ireland. The lands were granted to the Wingfield family, later Viscounts Powerscourt, by James I in 1609, after a series of appeals by Richard Wingfield, Marshal of Ireland and a veteran of Irish and Continental wars. The intention was that Wingfield would secure the district from the incursions of the native Irish lords and the families who had previously occupied the territory.

As an important strategic location the area had been a stronghold successively of le Poers – who gave the modern name to this district – O'Tooles, FitzGeralds and non-resident Talbots before the arrival of the Wingfields. It may have been with some appreciation of the need for the castle's original defensive strengths that, on modernizing his newly inherited residence in 1728, another Richard Wingfield, later Viscount Powerscourt of the 3rd creation, incorporated in the new building a significant part of the existing fabric.

The destruction by fire of the house's interiors revealed in the exposed fabric a history of special interest, and confirmed that Powerscourt was only one in a long line of modernizers of an ancient fabric. The original structure consisted of a low range incorporated in the two bays to the left of the entrance. This appears to have been a long, two-storey, rectangular block, raised to a third storey in later development, and retaining, in one corner, a cross-shaped angle loop. The vaulted room on the ground floor in this range survived into later remodellings. This earliest block, which dates from no later than the fifteenth century, was extended by a connecting block now incorporated in the garden front and, finally, by a third rectangular range fronted by the two bays on the right of the entrance, creating a U-plan.

Christopher Hussey did not have the advantage of the archaeological evidence revealed after the firing of the central block three decades later, but he was able to provide a remarkably prescient summary of the building's history alongside an acute analysis of its design.

Hussey recognized immediately the distinctive inspiration for the classical features in the final design: 'The great scale and broad simplicity of the shaping are grand in the true sense … giving to the front the massive dignity of a great Italian Renaissance villa'.

Preceding pages: *Gill's views of the lost entrance hall, located below the saloon, and the surviving exterior, capture well the rich culture of Powerscourt.*

Left: *The side of the garden front highlights the change in scale between the three-storey medieval castle to the right and the later range facing the garden.*

The new residence, given the variety of its incorporated fabric, was never intended to be a pristine piece of perfect Palladianism, but a vigorous, sturdy and secure country residence. It did more to suggest an open classical disposition than it did to effect it, and took its inspiration from the great villas of the Roman Renaissance even more than from Palladio's Venetian work. In a Roman villa the impression of power and the fact of security were equally vital, while the specific Venetian sources for Powerscourt probably were even less important than the Scottish. As the Knight of Glin later observed, formal sources for much of the detailing might be found in the designs of the great Scottish architect William Adam, father of the brothers Adam.

When the building was developed in the eighteenth century the real challenge became the incorporation of the new within the old.

Left: *The staircase hall, in an unpublished view, with its classical decoration, romantic portraits and exotic Austrian* Lüsterweiblen *or antler chandelier. The room, now destroyed, was located in the latest of the three wings of a pre-Georgian complex.*

Above: *The large drawing room, adjoining the saloon, was set into the existing garden range, even providing a classical enfilade, as captured by Gill in 1946.*

Windows were adjusted and regularized, and masses harmonized, all with sufficient regard for the original fabric to inspire the criticism levied by the *Georgian Society Records*. Yet one part of the building did succeed in surpassing all precedent, and any criticism: the central saloon which was created in the open court formed by the U-plan of the older house. Such ingenuity allowed for the creation of a classical space unhampered by the pre-Georgian structure, indeed one supported by it. It would only be with Robert Adam's proposed insertion of a rotunda in the courtyard at Syon House, London, that architecture in these islands would encounter again a scheme of such imagination, and Adam's was never executed.

The articulation of the saloon followed in exemplary fashion progressive neo-Palladian practice. The space was developed from the so-called 'Egyptian Hall', a form derived from ancient Roman authority and revived in the Renaissance, most notably by Palladio. It was to become a popular form in the eighteenth century, but was still very progressive in the 1730s. In England, Lord Burlington, leader of the neo-Palladians, also explored this form, but in public building, not private. The execution of this monumental work was

not as expensive as might first appear, for the huge columns were only painted to give the effect of yellow Siena marble – though it should be remembered, too, that they were cut out of huge monoliths of granite.

Perhaps the most unusual of the rooms was the entrance hall, located immediately below the saloon. Its low ceiling allowed for the creation of the magnificent rise of the two-storey saloon, without lifting it so high as to destroy the skyline of the entrance front. The proportions of the hall were also determined by the width of the open court in which it sat. Thus it became a space of almost daunting character, low and broad, but magnificently relieved by the chaos of the antlers, on stags' heads – stuffed or made of papier-mâché – and sprouting from chandeliers.

The only major room not to be recorded by Gill was an early eighteenth-century domed and panelled interior situated in the corner tower beside the original castle. In this case Hussey's eye failed him for he incorrectly ascribed it to 1835 – from the need to date the wing more than the interior – and missed clear evidence of its early Georgian origin. Indeed, the quirky combination of clear classical columns and luscious baroque detail – highlighted by inversely tapering pilasters – recalls the first floor of the hall at Castletown. Given this, and the supreme ingenuity of the arrangement of the saloon, the involvement of Sir Edward Lovett Pearce in some aspects of the design of Powerscourt cannot be excluded, despite the absence of any known reference to him in the unusually copious documentation.

Outside the house, it is the terraces at the rear of the building that impress most. The gardens seen today are largely a creation of the nineteenth century, combining the inventive design of the Scottish émigré architect Daniel Robertson and his successor F. C. Penrose, and the patronage and ideas of the 6th and 7th Viscounts. Their terraced effect, however, derives from an early eighteenth-century – or earlier – layout, possibly associated with Richard Castle. Original maps of the estate document the sweep of the land from the house down to the pool, an informal conclusion to the more architectonic structure of the progression of terraces.

Hussey went to some pains to document the charitable activities of the then Lord and Lady Powerscourt, including free public access to the estate. The family's contribution to the progress of a modern Ireland was considerable, though in more recent years the house, after being exposed to the elements since its burning, has seen further construction and development, and much surviving material has been lost.

This view of the saloon was left unpublished in favour of a less extravagant version, probably because of the prominence of the Victorian accretions in the classical space, including the fireplace and the Italian baroque gilded chandeliers, part of the 7th Viscount's purchase from a Bolognese palazzo.

Overleaf: *The gardens, looking towards the circular pool (formerly Juggy's Pond), were mostly developed in the nineteenth century from formal Renaissance gardens, following designs by Daniel Robertson and F. C. Penrose.*

ELEVEN

TOWNLEY HALL

Co LOUTH

Hussey's enthusiasm for the abstract power of Francis Johnston's Townley Hall encouraged an unusual approach.
He reported on the building's spatial climax before turning, in the second article, to explain the history of the house. The progress into
the curvilinear staircase hall from the rectilinear entrance hall is indeed one of the great moments of Irish classical architecture,
and urged from Hussey a plaudit with which many would agree: 'I would dare say there is nothing lovelier than this rotunda in
the Georgian architecture of the British Isles'. The contrast of sweeping curve and straight line inside the house is anticipated outside,
but inversely, and only in the most subtle fashion. Here the rigid formality of the stone box of Townley is offset against the
rolling landscape, pitted with bulbous clumps of trees modulating the already undulating horizon.

The landscape itself is not untypical of the plains of northern Leinster's interior, the region in which the Townley estate sits. Located near the banks of the River Boyne in Co. Louth, and not far from the scene of the titular battle, it came to Blaney Townley-Balfour on the death of his grandfather in 1788.

It was in the years before his marriage in 1797 to Lady Florence Cole, daughter of the 1st Earl of Enniskillen, that the young gentleman planned and commenced a building that would come to represent a whole new phase in the history of Irish architecture. His Townley Hall, designed and built in the 1790s, could stand proudly beside the greatest house then being built in the country, Castlecoole, Co. Fermanagh, situated only a county westward. Furthermore, being designed by a young Irish architect of obvious talent, Francis Johnston, the new house instigated an enthusiasm for the work of native architects that would carry into the following century.

Hussey wrote of the house's 'remarkable … essentially Irish classicism – as contrasted with that of the alien architects' so often employed in Ireland. Throughout the building, austerity and structural rationalism combine to produce a style imbued with

contemporary Grecian taste, but evocative too of the mood of early Christian builders in Ireland, for whom architecture was the simple expression of structural logic.

In the staircase hall itself may be found the simple expression – however difficult the execution – of the fundamental structure of the cantilevered stone staircase. One of the great developments in Irish Georgian architecture, and well represented also in the staircase at Castletown, Co. Kildare, this principle consists of stone slabs – the steps – wedged into a supporting wall, without support for their projecting ends. At Townley, Johnston takes full advantage of the slightness such a treatment will allow to give an especially open effect in the rotunda of the staircase hall. This pure space, measuring roughly ten metres by fourteen, with coffered

Preceding pages: *Westley's views of the central staircase hall and the exterior, the latter unpublished. The glazing bars, disguised by their dark paint, do not soften its geometry.*

These pages: *The entrance hall* (above) *includes original furnishings, many now dispersed, such as the curved settees in the shallow niches. The first-floor landing* (right), *again in an unpublished view, is integrated with lobbies behind arches, feeding to the rooms, a variation of the Irish top-lit circulation lobby.*

ceiling and panelled walls, is twisted through by the sweeping visual corkscrew of the staircase, showing how good architecture can become great.

Assimilated into this majestic staircase hall is a distinctively Irish arrangement, the top-lit first-floor landing of the type found at Russborough. Hussey published his own schematic drawing in order to explain how the top of the staircase gave access to the first-floor rooms through rectangular lobbies extending from the curved landing in the hall proper. However, he did not refer to the pattern as a development from the Irish lobby arrangement, though it might be contrasted easily with the more architectonic – if less imaginative – variant at Castlecoole.

Johnston's design for Townley Hall also displayed an apparently natural appreciation of progressive country house design. Outside, he eschews unnecessary ornament, and creates a building which rises like some classical temple directly from the ground – without

The drawing room (above) has superb Chinese wallpaper, probably obtained through Townley-Balfour's brother-in-law, Arthur Cole. With nothing other than the glass above dado level, the integrity of the paper is preserved, while the absence of ceiling lamps unifies the space. In the library (left) books perform the role of the paper, while the paintwork may be original.

the intercession of steps, area or a raised basement – as the best of contemporary taste required. Inside, continuing the mood, a sequence of vast pure spaces regulated by proportion and shallow ornament renders the very flow between rooms into the poetry of the architecture.

Though it is a building of apparent simplicity, in fact Townley Hall is one of ingenious duplicity. Behind its tall cornice hides a pitched roof of sufficient scale to hold an attic lit by dormers, while below its earthen base lies another floor. This, and more, is revealed at the rear, where in addition to the actual four-storey elevation is found the discreetly hidden kitchen wing and court. This last, an aspect of the modern convenience that always clouded the primitive aspirations of the most intense neoclassical patrons and architects, is the only part of the exterior to receive arches.

Francis Johnston was a pupil of Thomas Cooley and, after the building of Townley Hall, he soon came to establish himself as Ireland's finest native-born architect since Sir Edward Lovett Pearce. Yet the commission for Blaney Townley-Balfour was not gained lightly. His patron looked for designs first, in 1792, from the noted Scottish neoclassicist James Playfair. Playfair records in his diaries the completion of his designs in July of that year, the work

having been requested at a meeting in Rome the previous April. However, by 1794 Johnston had been decided upon as the new architect, and was soon able to supply a detailed estimate for the proposed house. The degree to which Johnston relied on the designs of the Scottish master is uncertain. What is clear is that a number of features explored by Playfair persist in Johnston's work, from the use of seven-bay elevations to details in the kitchen court and even the door panelling – this last has a close parallel at Playfair's own Cairness, Aberdeenshire. The cornices may be best compared to those of Johnston's master Thomas Cooley at Caledon. Regardless of this, however, the character of the building has been made very much his own.

Johnston's estimate of £10,473, exclusive of decoration, was substantial, especially considering the lack of elaboration typical of this phase of neoclassicism. Much of the expense was due to a tireless sophistication of detail and the emphasis given to the provision of modern facilities. Townley, exceptional for its day, was equipped with running water, and the surviving drawings include a plan of these services.

It is especially fortunate that a number of original documents and drawings survive, many now held in the Irish Architectural Archive in Dublin. The mason is identified as John Glover of nearby Drogheda, but there is no record of the decorators who supplied the furnishings, and many of these may have been supplied through the architect.

Following the death of Mrs Townley-Balfour in 1954, widow of the grandson of Blaney Townley-Balfour and resident during the time of Hussey's visit, it passed to David Crichton, from whom it was purchased by Trinity College Dublin in 1956, to serve as its first school of agriculture. It has more recently been in the possession of a private institution. Unfortunately, little of its original furniture survives and the kitchen wing, beautifully documented by Westley, has been gutted.

Above: *The kitchen wing, hidden to the rear of the house, has its own court, and its external detailing registers Johnston's debt to the Scottish architect who produced the first designs for the house, James Playfair. The kitchen, since gutted, has a curved gallery intended for hanging meat.*

Right: *The attic dormitories are carefully detailed – note the curved fans to the corners over the window shutters – marking its original formal use as a barracks for the male visitors.*

TWELVE

BEAULIEU

Co LOUTH

The account of Beaulieu given by Mark Girouard marked the reopening of *Country Life*'s interest in Irish houses after an interregnum which had lasted much of the 1950s. Beaulieu also represented both the wider stylistic interests and the slightly smaller scale of house that would be more typical of this phase of the journal's coverage. These interests had been anticipated during Hussey's days, for the photographs of Beaulieu were taken by Westley in 1947, twelve years before Girouard's articles, and would have been intended for a piece by Hussey himself.

In Ireland the modern appreciation of post-medieval architecture coincided with the rise of interest in Georgian design. Buildings erected outside the Georgian period proper could be overlooked. Public works such as the Royal Hospital at Kilmainham, Dublin, lost houses such as Eyrecourt in Galway, and rare surviving gems such as Beaulieu all have a baroque heaviness and architectural detailing that had a somewhat narrower appeal. Later seventeenth-century houses in Ireland could be less elaborate and more rugged than their more numerous and varied English counterparts, and held rather less immediate attraction.

It was only with the recognition of the rarity of such work in Ireland, and the appreciation of its very special characteristics, that places such as Beaulieu gained a more appreciative recognition. Hussey, in intending to write up Beaulieu, having seen it in Sadleir and Dickinson's *Georgian Mansions* of 1915, would have recognized its importance as a rare Irish representative of the period. However, it is fitting that it should have been the successor at *Country Life* to Hussey's Irish interests, Mark Girouard, who brought this building again to the attention of the British, and the Irish, public.

Beaulieu, situated just beside the River Boyne near Drogheda, sits on land historic in its own right. It came into the possession of

the man who built the house, Sir Henry Tichborne, from an old and famous Anglo-Irish family, the Plunketts, as spoils of war – though by tradition he is supposed to have purchased it. Tichborne, later 1st Baron Ferrard, was an ingenious soldier who succeeded, reputedly with only seventeen hundred men, in holding off ten times that number in the siege of Drogheda during the Catholic rebellion of 1641–2. On the estate's own lands Tichborne had also won some important smaller victories, but he gained title to them only on the Restoration, the rights being offered to him in consideration of his fundamental loyalty to the Crown despite the fact that he had previously fought against it. Perhaps it was in recognition of the confused waste of war that the new home he built there carried no significant defences.

Preceding pages: *The two-storey hall, as photographed by Westley, is a living space in the medieval manner, hiding behind the classical exterior of the west, entrance front.*

These pages: *The front to the river* (below) *continues the early classical features of steep roof, dormer windows, tall stacks and symmetrical composition. The wall of the hall* (right) *presents an historical* résumé, *including portraits, late seventeenth-century chairs and a mid-eighteenth-century table.*

Constructed some time after about 1660, Beaulieu was among the first and finest of a small vanguard of regular, non-defensive seventeenth-century houses to be built in Ireland. Though it was originally more enclosed than it appears today – in 1830 it was surrounded by a palisade which may have dated from the 1660s – the present layout indicates the modernity of Tichborne's home. The effect is enhanced by the development of the gardens away from the house and the setting of grass terraces about a secondary elevation, looking to the river. The emphatic rejection of defensive measures extended even to forgoing the building of an area, the acceptable Georgian variation of the moat.

The classical interests and civilized character of the exterior continue inside the house, and where the gesture of the warrior does appear, it is subordinated as decorative device. In the entrance hall the magnificence impresses itself on the visitor through architectural effect – the grandeur of the way it rises through two storeys, with the upper levels glazed, most unusually, on inner and outer walls. The internal windows, like those outside with sashes postdating the original construction, allow light to pass between the corridor and hall, and repeat an arrangement found also at the only slightly earlier French baroque château of Vaux-le-Vicomte.

The hall is interesting especially for its suggestion of the mixture of traditional or medieval and new Renaissance lifestyles. It is backward looking in the conception of a hall as public living room, a function it continues to serve today as it takes up such a huge proportion of the building, as suggested by Westley's photographs. Yet the hall also looks ahead to the Renaissance in its classical articulation and its enforced symmetry, all symbolizing the power of intellectual discipline.

Ignoring the ubiquitous antlers, and regretting the frieze of lincrusta swags, Girouard was impressed by treasures including the arrangement of pictures, furnishings and swords along the south wall of the hall. Here were portraits of Mrs Tipping and her daughter, and Maria and Sidney Montgomery, all associated with the later history of the house. These, together with some

Above: The view from the drawing room across the hall encapsulates the coherent design of Tichborne's seventeenth-century house, though this photograph was not published. The heavy bolection mouldings on the wall panelling are typical of the period.

Right: The dining room has deep square openings for the windows, bolection-moulded panelling and door surround, and compartmented ceiling, all rare survivals from the seventeenth century.

enthusiastically ornamented furniture, were all arranged below a portrait of William of Orange, of which only the lower part of the frame appeared.

The living rooms of the house, though altered in places, have survived remarkably well in their original form. This is especially surprising considering the unsettled years and changing tastes Ireland faced in the centuries after the house was built. The drawing-room ceiling, deeply framed and compartmented, is especially noticeable considering the size of the room, and even won that rarest of items in Ireland, its intended painting. Here, in true baroque fashion, and recalling the great ceiling paintings of Rome, the view shows an architectural scene framing a view to a cherub-dappled sky, with clouds suggesting space, and sculpture for antique effect. Girouard thought the painting to be in the style of Verrio, who popularized this form of decoration.

Ireland is fortunate that Beaulieu has, since Girouard's article, not only survived, but also been improved. It is to the great credit of its owner, Mrs Nesbit Waddington, that this fine house and its wonderful setting continue to give pleasure to its many admirers.

Left: *The staircase, with Corinthian newels, dates to about 1720. Girouard surmised that it replaced the original, but, like Castletown, the house might not have gained its main staircase until long after the building was concluded. The window looks into the hall.*

This page: *The drawing room. The ceiling painting* (top) *is 'in the style popularised by Verrio', and the chimney-piece* (above) *is a late Georgian insertion featuring Neptune.*

133

THIRTEEN

CHARLEVILLE FOREST

Co OFFALY

When Mark Girouard published his short notice of Charleville Forest in September 1962 it must have been a revelation for the readers of *Country Life*, not only for the extraordinary scale of the interiors, but for its lavish finish in a Georgian Gothic style. When Girouard had these interiors photographed the house was vacant, and the empty rooms had to be specially furnished with items borrowed from nearby Belvedere House, in Co. Westmeath.

Charleville Forest is situated in Ireland's midlands, the fertile lands lying far from the quixotic influence of sea trade, in an area that is often swayed by a powerful personality or strong imagination. Set within striking distance of the town of Tullamore, and surrounded by clusters of deciduous trees and yew walks, these last dating perhaps to the 1850s, its tall, battlemented stone towers reach irregularly and with great natural effect above the skyline. Though rising at their tallest to some one hundred and twenty-five feet, they give a surprisingly ineffective suggestion of the medieval castle, for their medievalism is rooted less in the sporadic construction of the so-called Dark Ages than in the tweaking of a largely symmetrical Georgian house.

Charleville Forest's patron, Charles William Bury, from 1800 Viscount and from 1806 Earl of Charleville, was a man well versed in contemporary English taste and style. He inherited lands in Limerick, through his father's maternal line, and in Offaly. His great wealth, lavish lifestyle and generous nature allowed him simultaneously to distribute largesse in Ireland, live grandly in London and travel widely on the Continent. Such experience provided the spur to the building of his new house at Tullamoore – as it then was – to replace the outdated seventeenth-century house, known as Redwood, located by the river.

Following the only serious alternative taste to that of the Grecian neoclassial, Bury turned towards the picturesque effect that might be gained from the medieval castle style. Though far from the first Irish house to adopt this style, Charleville Forest was to confirm the viability of the Gothic style for those wanting to evoke associations of historic lines, ancient days and mysterious ages. Bury adopted the castle style not, as had often been the case, because of the incorporation of existing medieval fabric, but gratuitously, simply to suggest a Gothic past in a wholly new building. In this he anticipated the myriad of pseudo-Gothic villas that would spring up in Ireland's city suburbs in later generations, though Bury's was on a significantly more impressive scale.

Bury's intention, as he wrote in his own unfinished account of the work, was to 'exhibit specimens of Gothic architecture' adapted to 'chimneypieces, ceilings, windows, balustrades etc.', but without excluding 'convenience and modern refinements in luxury'. This recipe for the Georgian Gothic villa had already been used at Horace Walpole's Strawberry Hill in London, and Bury's cultivated lifestyle in England certainly would have made him aware of that house and its long line of descendants.

It may be that Bury himself – possibly with the assistance of his wife – outlined some of the more dramatic features in his new house, as is suggested by a number of drawings relating to the final design which still survive, now in the Irish Architectural Archive in Dublin. These all show the crude hand of an amateur, but equally betray a total freedom of imagination unshackled by the discipline of architectural training. In particular, a drawing of the exterior shows the smaller tower rising up out of the ground like a tree, with its base spreading and separating as it grows into the ground like roots.

It was the architect, Francis Johnston, who gave to these fantastic drawings the professional finish that distinguishes the executed work. Johnston had already proved his skill in the classical style at Townley Hall, Co. Louth, though he had only limited experience of Gothic when he was called in to work on this new house. Johnston's involvement probably dates to about 1800, as the earliest drawing appears to be a basement plan dated February 1801. From this time on, Johnston's practice in the Gothic style, made increasingly popular no doubt by the success of Charleville Forest, expanded rapidly. Work here progressed slowly, however, not least because of Johnston's continuing professional success, highlighted by his appointment to the Board of Works in 1805. The year before, Johnston agreed with Charleville that 'things went on too slow at the castle', but by the end of 1812 a limited amount of work was still in progress.

Yet by 1809 the house was officially open for public display, as the family entertained the Viceroy, the Duke of Richmond, and his wife. Lady Charleville recorded the 'magnificent full-dress liveries … for the servants, and a uniform of Blue and Scarlet for the upper men', and the event was orchestrated without heed of cost. Lord Charleville's real objective, however, the lucrative post of the Irish Postmastership for which he applied soon after and in which he might have expected some assistance from his recent guests, did not come to him.

Preceding pages: *The entrance front, and as seen along one of the radial yew walks. Despite its contrasting towers, it remains essentially symmetrical and therefore classical.*

These pages: *The visitor is confronted by unexpected grandeur in the entrance hall (right). The single straight flight of stairs rises to the classically inspired piano nobile. Starkey captures well a softer side with his view of the boudoir (above), its light plaster vault confirmation that Charleville was a castle born of Georgian frivolity.*

Charleville's lack of success in his search for a sinecure proved ill for the future of the family fortunes for, continuing to live extravagantly above their means, they advanced speedily towards bankruptcy. On Charleville's death in 1835 the estate was 'embarrassed', and by 1844 the Limerick estates had to be sold and the castle shut up, while his son and heir, 'the greatest bore the world can produce' according to one contemporary, retired to Berlin.

Johnston's designs for Charleville Forest, encouraged if not actually inspired by the ideas of his patron and his family, captured perfectly the combination of Gothic taste and modern comfort that was to distinguish the pre-Victorian Gothic revival. His interiors, on the surface varied through wildly different manners of plaster ornament, were wrought inside an otherwise static square box. Its rectangular rooms he contracted or attenuated, and its overall shape he enlivened with irregular towers, but he never failed to follow an underlying classical order and uniformity. Such a sentimental fondness for regularity, which pervades all his Gothic work, is to be expected of the architect of Townley Hall.

In enriching his Gothic designs, Johnston also often added a thread of Irish tradition. Later, at the Chapel Royal in Dublin Castle, he placed a Celtic cross over its east window, one of the earliest examples of an architect's interest in the Celtic revival. At Charleville Forest we find a comparable treatment, as he recreates double-stepped battlements often associated with a specifically Irish tradition, although these gestures were, almost invariably, confined to details.

Externally the house, with its tall central tower rising over the main body, finds its precedent in the work of English architects – in Roger Morris's castle at Inverary, Argyllshire, built in 1746, and probably Morris's own inspiration, Robert Smythson's Wollaton Hall. The entrance hall, with the exotic melodrama of its staircase, may have been conceived in its entirety by Bury. A crudely drawn section describing its arrangement in surprisingly accurate detail still survives. An immediate model may have been Wyatt's recent Gothic entrance hall at Fonthill Abbey, Wiltshire, begun in 1795, which had attracted much attention thanks to the notoriety of its patron, William Beckford. However, both Charleville and Fonthill have their own precedent in the entrance hall of William Kent's neo-Palladian Holkham Hall, Norfolk, of about 1734.

The other main interiors in the castle, though largely exemplary Georgian Gothic, offer little more than a restatement of the starting point for most castles of this type, Walpole's Strawberry Hill. Johnston's work may be on a larger scale and have the benefit of additional antiquarian experience, but the mood, and sometimes even the arrangement, is comparable. The long gallery, reached at

The gallery was described by Girouard as 'perhaps the most splendid example of a Gothic interior in Ireland'. Designed by the architect Francis Johnston, for its date it is rivalled only by his contemporary designs for the Gothic Chapel Royal at Dublin Castle.

the head of the staircase and spreading itself across the garden front, is a derivation from that in Strawberry Hill, but has an additional Irish precedent in Pearce's classical gallery at Castletown, Co Kildare. The impressive scale of Johnston's gallery gives it a more substantial form than might be expected, particularly its surprisingly broad proportions. Johnston is also careful to co-ordinate the articulation of wall and vaulting, as doors, fireplaces and windows are framed by the clustered shafts that carry, visually at least, the spreading ribs of the fan vault. The treatment recurs successfully in the hall, but the absence of a comparable arrangement in the dining room destroys any possible link between the classical shape and the Gothic details, and even

the impressive medievalism of the chimney-piece, inspired by the west door of Magdalen College Chapel, Oxford, fails to disguise the essential classicism of this space.

Despite the monumental grandeur of Charleville Forest, or perhaps because of it, its history has been largely less than happy. The 3rd Earl returned to the house in 1851, but with a much reduced fortune; the property was then inherited by his grand-daughter Lady Emily Howard-Bury, after whose death in 1931 it remained unoccupied, as it was at the time of Girouard's article. Later it was let to M. G. McMullen, who secured its immediate future and began its restoration. More recently it has been purchased for development in a commercial venture.

Left: *The main staircase, leading to the upper floors, is somewhat cramped due to the massive scale of the entrance hall. However, there is no sparing of the light Gothic trim that pervades the main rooms of the house, which continues even under the stairs.*

Above: *The dining room retains the proportions of a classical interior, a feature accentuated by the borrowed furniture. The ceiling, with its coffered panels, sports family emblems of the Moores and the Burys, all supported on a light Gothic crested frieze, dating to 1875 and a remnant of William Morris's only Irish commission.*

FOURTEEN

CURRAGHMORE

Co WATERFORD

Public notices of Curraghmore are rare. Charles Smith, in his *Ancient and Present State of the County and City of Waterford*, published in 1746, provided an early description of the house as it then stood, recording an old tower to which a house was added in 1700, 'which date is on the pedestal of the door-case'. The house was reported on briefly by the *Georgian Society Records* in 1913, and more fully in *Georgian Mansions* of 1915. Mark Girouard, writing in *Country Life* in 1963, brought its distinctive mixture of structural and decorative styles to a wider public.

Of the many curious and distinguishing features to be found at Curraghmore, among the most striking is the courtyard front of the house, where the original castle is encased in a Victorian classical confection designed by S. A. Roberts.

It is surprising how effective the composition is, and it may well be the survival or revival of interest in Vanbrugh's architecture at the time, in conjunction with the dramatic massing deriving from the re-use of the medieval core, that ensured Curraghmore's remarkable aesthetic success – immediately recognizable and undeniably moving.

Contributing to its success is the vibrant classical frame provided by the mid-Georgian architect responsible for the ranges flanking the castle itself, vigorously composed and enjoyably varied throughout. The architect of this and the other mid-eighteenth-century remodelling is unknown, but the name of a talented and local Waterford architect, John Roberts, is mentioned most frequently by historians, though they freely admit a lack of documentary authority for the attribution.

This work, together with the internal remodelling, was carried out by the last heir to carry the Power name at Curraghmore, Lady Catherine Power, only child of the 3rd and last Earl of Tyrone of the 1st creation, and her husband, Marcus Beresford, 1st Earl of Tyrone of the 2nd creation. The Powers, or le Poers to give the family its more correct name, had successfully built up their Waterford estates in the centuries following the Norman invasion.

Here, not far from the Comeragh mountains, they carved out a little pocket kingdom for themselves in this fertile and temperate part of south-eastern Ireland.

Feuding on occasion with the city of Waterford, and only rarely pitted against more powerful opponents, they maintained a comparatively comfortable security, and held their estates during that most disruptive of centuries in Ireland, the seventeenth. When so many lost their estates due to Catholic affirmation or Royalist inclination, the Curraghmore le Poers remained safely aloof and made no alliances. This was not necessarily due to astute politics, and certainly it was assisted by the lunacy of John, Lord le Poer, whose insanity had been recognized many years before the outbreak of the civil wars.

Preceding pages: *The entrance hall at Curraghmore, inside the original medieval castle, redecorated in about 1750, and the approach which, in scale, is comparable to Vanbrugh's Blenheim.*

These pages: *Two unpublished views by Starkey: the billiard room* (right), *with its curious screen of early Georgian Corinthian columns on tall circular pedestals set into the medieval fabric, and the yellow drawing room* (above), *part of the late eighteenth-century work by Wyatt. The carpet is also Georgian.*

With the eighteenth century, and Lady Catherine's successful alliance with Sir Marcus Beresford, the family and estates secured for themselves a more outward-looking future and a substantial joint fortune that raised them to the ranks of the richest in Ireland. They soon set about the remodelling of their seat. Extensions to make the original castle more habitable had been documented as early as 1654, when it was described as 'a fayre castle and a goodly stone house', presumably a new structure attached to the rear of the castle. It had been developed further in about 1700, and contained a staircase, ornamented by Johann van der Hagen, that was described by Smith as having 'columns, festoons etc., between which are several landscapes' and a ceiling 'in perspective ... a Dome, the columns seeming to rise, though on a flat surface'.

If the style of some surviving features, such as the courtyard, might suggest a degree of provincialism, the quality of the craftsmanship secured the house's artistic success. The courtyard is an especially successful example of the mixture of late baroque and neo-Palladian detailing, one characteristic of the decades about the mid-eighteenth century throughout Ireland. Lady Beresford herself

decorated the inside of a shell house, under construction during Smith's visit, and surviving today, which suggests her especially enthusiastic appreciation of its rococo fancy.

It was the 2nd Earl, afterwards 1st Marquess of Waterford, who was responsible for the next phase of modernization, which included perhaps some of the most important interiors to survive. He replaced the extension of about 1700 in the 1780s, creating a suite of rooms that together capture perfectly the tasteful restraint of the later eighteenth century. He ensured its fashionable success by securing James Wyatt as his architect. Wyatt, the prolific contemporary of the Adam brothers and talented copyist of their

Left: An unpublished view of Wyatt's staircase hall, a perfect prelude to his Irish work of the 1790s. The plaster decoration continues the manner of the 1770s and may be contrasted with Wyatt's more reserved style, a decade later, at Castlecoole.

Above: The dining room was used for the visit of Prince William Henry, later William IV, in 1787. Wyatt's responsibility for the work was confirmed by the discovery of a group of his drawings for the house in the Metropolitan Museum, New York.

style, was already in 1785 gathering to himself a cluster of Irish commissions as he toured the country. At Curraghmore he developed a series of rooms considered by many to be among his most successful in Ireland.

Wyatt was an imaginative architect, but often careless, and through laxity and mismanagement succeeded in gaining for himself a professional reputation unequalled in England for its disparagement. However, in Ireland his designs actually benefited from his absence, as they were carried out by Irish architects, clerks or craftsman, all with rather more professional integrity than the architect. Consequently Wyatt's Irish work has a character and a beauty all its own, and at Curraghmore, that combination of absentee architect and careful craftsmanship reached its highest expression.

After Wyatt's Georgian developments, work at Curraghmore in the nineteenth century concentrated on the gardens, and the Victorian refacing and refronting outside. Daniel Robertson, who worked also on the gardens at Powerscourt, prepared designs in 1833 for Gothicizing the building, but these were rejected. Instead, the less familiar figure of S. A. Roberts applied the features seen in the central block. These are centred on the Stag of St Hubert, with the cross between its antlers, which was executed by Queen Victoria's favourite sculptor, Sir Joseph Edgar Boehm. Boehm was responsible also for the haunting representation of the deceased first wife of the 5th Marquess, who died in childbirth, and which survives in the family chapel at Clonegam.

In the nineteenth century the medieval castle range found its rooms further rearranged in response to Wyatt's extension; they also took on their own special, more informal character. Fortunately, however, they retained their mid-eighteenth-century decoration. The entrance hall, with its barrel-vaulted ceiling covered in rather light classical plaster decoration, is dominated by a huge family portrait. Dating to about 1760, it shows the Earl and his Countess – formerly Lady Catherine Power and the heiress to Curraghmore – with their family. The space is also filled with a profusion of trophies, these belonging mostly to the 6th Marquess of Waterford. The room above the entrance hall was transformed into a billiard room, happily by no more serious a procedure than inserting a billiard table.

The later history of the fabric of Curraghmore, fortunately, is lacking in event, and Girouard's and Starkey's record of the house, though made as late as 1963, shows a rare cluster of interiors of the highest order still fully furnished. The house remains to this day intact and in the possession of the family, a phenomenon decidedly rare in Ireland.

The blue drawing room with ceiling decoration attributed to Antonio Zucchi for the lunettes and, for the grisaille border roundels depicting cupids at play, Peter de Gree, who may also have painted the wall panels in the dining room.

FIFTEEN

HUMEWOOD CASTLE

Co WICKLOW

Humewood Castle, one of the most impressive of all Victorian country houses, sits comfortably in an unexpectedly gentle part of Wicklow,
near its Kildare border. Despite its evident grandeur, the designer, the English church architect William White, considered it
'a work which did not aspire to be classed above the ordinary average of a small-sized family mansion'. Furthermore its patron,
W. W. F. Hume Dick MP, owner of houses in London and France, thought of it more as an occasional summer lodge. This was about
as close as the two ever got to agreement. Such inconsistencies were bound to lead to trouble, and Humewood became the focus
of one of the most famous legal actions in nineteenth-century professional architectural circles.

The case centred on the agreement between architect and client that the house would not cost more than £15,000, when in fact it ended up costing some £25,000. The builder, Albert Kimberley of Banbury, sought and gained legal recourse against architect and client after Dick refused to pay more than the agreed sum. In 1876, on the conclusion of this widely reported action, one journal, the *Architect*, remarked that 'the most striking feature in the case is the rashness and lack of caution displayed by all parties concerned'. Perhaps such rashness was especially likely when architect and builder had little knowledge of Ireland, and the patron only a little more.

It is unfortunate that the house should be better known for the confusion of its contractual agreements than for the genius of its design. For Humewood is not only a house with few equals in either Britain or Ireland, it is also one of the small number of secular commissions by a talented and eccentric architect more used to simple church spaces, and all the more willing to explore new approaches in domestic design.

Humewood strikes us as being different outside, first because it lifts itself up on a tall basement, an arrangement considered old-fashioned in most circles but justified by White as avoiding damp from the ground and providing better views. It also provided extra security for the residents, as Wicklow, with the protection provided by its mountains, had always been a district prone to revolutionary uprisings. In the troubled decades of the 1860s and 1870s, such considerations were all the more important.

The exterior of the building is dominated by its continually varying roof line, a response to White's own observation that 'For exterior effect our attention must be directed to the sky outline'. Yet the use of steep roofs, stepped gables and caps to bay-window projections might also be seen as no more than responses to issues of structure or internal planning: such variety allowed him to lower the height of the building towards the service end to the north, and to raise the grand tower over the entrance and staircase hall, which could carry water tanks for the household.

Preceding pages: Gibson's photographs, including an unpublished view of the side, capture the domestic masterpiece of an architect also known for inventions such as the springless lock and the wasteless lavatory.

These pages: Inside, the low ribbed stone vaulting (below) in this unpublished photograph confirms the architect's familiarity with church architecture. The view into the staircase hall (right), with heraldic stained glass and a vigorous contrast of stone column and nude, slowly dispels ecclesiastical associations.

White's practical nature is evident, too, in his treatment of the exterior masonry, composed entirely of granite, although at one time banding with brick was considered. The simple massing and plain surfaces, with windows unrelieved by surrounds or decorative tracery, leaves only the eventful buttress, the occasional broadly profiled corbel course, string or coping to the stepped gables, or the rare battlemented machicoulis to model the wall surface. The effect is continued in the stable court, situated to the north-east of the main house to minimize odours, where the stepped gables, plain window recesses and broad masses reveal that sensitivity to abstract qualities which gives White's church architecture such strength.

Left: The secondary staircase, leading to the bedroom floor above, and peering to the main staircase hall below, is executed in timber, in acknowledgement of its less formal role; this is also suggestive of Norwegian churches.

Above: The drawing room, looking west to the gardens and fields beyond. The painted ceilings are by the Italian artist Grispini, and the original book of designs still survives. It also holds sketches for a medieval tournament in the park.

Throughout the exterior this severe treatment is ideally suited to both the qualities of this hard stone and the labour required in its working, a talent honed by White's five years spent developing an architectural practice in Truro, Cornwall. His budget, despite overspending, always was considered 'strictly limited', and it is to his credit that the austerity of this detailing never appears impoverished. It should be remembered that it was the scale of the building, not its ornament, that caused White to overrun his estimate.

Girouard has pointed out that the reception rooms were by no means excessive, and already by about 1873 what had been nurseries were considered more suited to being changed into the present ballroom. This required the addition of a storey to the left of the garden front, softening subtly but significantly the drama of White's original, more emphatically triangular composition. The tall circular tower nearer the stables was built to house man-servants – safely segregated from the opposite sex. Both of these additions are the work of another English ecclesiastical architect, James Brooks.

As architectural expression, the internal arrangement at Humewood has few equals. It is centred on the progression from the entrance hall to the reception rooms leading off the connecting corridors. White's interest in creating stimulating vistas was rooted in the logical expression of these different spaces, overlapping and connecting through the circulation area of the staircase hall. One may suppose that, as the restrictions in church planning forced him to squeeze out of an internal space every ounce of its excitement, White seized the opportunity to exploit the complex interrelation of different spaces in a domestic interior. The thrilling internal picturesque is enlivened further by the profusion of unexpected events, from the framing of slightly risqué classical statues to the sprouting, at the heads and bases of the newel posts on the staircase, of curious carved knobs. Concerning this, one contemporary architectural critic astutely noted White's 'firm and muscular resolve to make everything crooked'.

Unfortunately, despite the absence of any criticism of the architect's taste, White's patron was not the person to overlook a gentleman's agreement on costs. His refusal to pay £10,000 more than he had expected, regardless of the magnificence and practical success of the design, would hardly have surprised anyone familiar with his family.

The Humes had played an active role in quelling the occasional rising that disturbed an otherwise largely uneventful but successful history. In the 1798 uprising, they formed the Humewood Cavalry, and the original house was garrisoned, but William Hume, head of the family and MP for the county, lost his life to the rebels. Despite the ultimate quelling of the rebellion, his son, William Hoare Hume, failed repeatedly to capture one of the most talented of the rebel leaders, Michael Dwyer – a latter-day Robin Hood who so impressed Hume that he bargained with the British government for Dwyer's safe passage to America should he surrender. This Dwyer did, but the deal was reneged on by the government, and he was deported to the more distant outpost of Australia. Hume, furious that his gentleman's bond had been broken, rode to Dublin and publicly slapped the man responsible for breaking the agreement. The family clearly always put great store by its word and, with White's failure to meet agreed costs on the new house built by William Hume's grandson, William Wentworth FitzWilliam Hume Dick, the results could only have been catastrophic.

In this century, too, the house has had a history not short of excitement, with the estate being reduced to the original eighteenth-century demesne by 1911, and more recently sold at auction after the death of Mme Mimi Hume-Weygand, to a syndicate that failed to pay its deposit. At present it is in private ownership, and development as a commercial venture is proposed.

The telling skyline was White's first concern, and he developed this making full use of the fall in land over the site. The original triangular composition was made more square with Brooks's extensions, raising the left side, but the walls remain busy with movement and windows.

SIXTEEN

ADARE MANOR

Co LIMERICK

Adare Manor was built as the seat of the Earls of Dunraven. The variety of its plan and details reflects the fact that it took over thirty years to build, involving a bewildering succession of builders, architects, masons and family members extending over two generations. The persistent interest in medieval styles, echoing the many ancient buildings in the area, emphasizes the strong local interests of the family, and gives the house and its builders a very special place in the history of Irish architecture.

Situated in the rich quiet lands straddling the River Maigue, south-west of the city of Limerick, the adjacent village of Adare is one of the most picturesque in the country, renowned for its elegant thatched cottages and its homely ambience. Nearby may be found a range of medieval monuments and monastic settlements especially abundant even for Ireland.

What one sees in the village today is mostly a more recent creation, though still some two centuries old. To understand its origins, one must turn towards Adare Manor. Occupying a gentle slope near the river, it sits on the same site as its early eighteenth-century predecessor, but its present character is very much a creation of the nineteenth century. The house was built in a complex succession of phases, all ably relayed by John Cornforth in *Country Life*, clarifying the published writings of the widow of the 2nd Earl and the original researches of the present Knight of Glin. The photographs, essential in explaining the complex history and layout of the house, were taken by Lord Rossmore, especially well known for his extensive record of Ireland's architectural heritage.

The original house at Adare was a composed, two-storey, steeply roofed early eighteenth-century classical block with dormers in the fashion of Beaulieu, Co. Louth, although with the addition of a pediment. It was raised by a storey later in the century, but eventually, if only gradually, superseded by a programme of new building undertaken by the 2nd and 3rd Earls of Dunraven. The family, the Quins, was one of the most distinguished of the old Irish families to succeed in the post-Norman era. Valentine Quin, a Catholic until 1739, when he registered as a Protestant, came into the lands at Adare, previously a FitzGerald estate, in 1703 and he probably was the builder of the classical house. His great-grandson, the 2nd Earl of Dunraven, was responsible for its replacement.

At the age of fifty, in 1832, Lord Dunraven finally was prevented by gout from following the favourite pastime of the Irish aristocrat, hunting. Instead he began to occupy himself with the building of a new house. His endeavour was supported by the substantial fortune of his wife Caroline, heiress of the Wyndhams of Dunraven, Glamorganshire, whose estate name he took in gratitude; his taste no doubt also profited by this alliance. Together the Dunravens developed a building that, perhaps because of limited professional involvement, could boast a number of highly original features. Furthermore, through the slow evolution of its design, with different architects contributing at different stages, the new house reflected well one characteristic of the Gothic style for, as in medieval times, at any point there appears to have been a genuine uncertainty about future intentions.

The first architect assisting at Adare, James Paine, was probably responsible for the shell of the early fabric alongside technical matters. The true drama of the building may have derived from the inspired and amateur interests of the Dunravens, and the energetic detailing provided by a succession of talented designers and craftsmen.

The ornamental carving at Adare is one of the earliest manifestations of a survival – or perhaps revival – in Ireland of ancient carving traditions. This same tradition would shape the future of the Gothic revival in Ireland, and make the nineteenth century one of the most creative periods in the whole history of the nation's architecture. Two names in particular are associated with the stonework over the 1830s and early 1840s, James Conolly and Michael Donoghue, but it remains uncertain as to which of them, if either, deserves the major credit. Nowhere is the creativity of Adare more apparent than in the Great Hall and its associated spaces. Enclosed by screens of giant and more modest arches, round and pointed, surrounded by corridors, staircases and steps flying in an apparently conflicting succession of directions, and with galleries breaking through walls, not to mention the ubiquitous antlers of the Irish elk, the great hall was one of the most picturesque interiors of its day. Lady Dunraven described the room as being 'peculiarly adapted to every purpose for which it may be required', observing that 'it has been frequently used with equal appropriateness as a dining-room, concert-room, ballroom, for private theatricals, *tableaux vivants* and other amusements'. Perhaps her sentiments reflect a personal pride in its success. Certainly it appears that the design itself, like so much of the rest of the house, evolved only slowly.

The hall evolved from more predictable designs by James Paine prepared in 1834, but it was still under development in 1846, when A. W. N. Pugin provided drawings. Despite the contribution by Pugin, an undisputed authority in the Gothic revival, the design clearly remained uninhibited by the decorum of any professional propriety, while much of it betrayed more of an ecclesiastical than a domestic character. Indeed, the arrangement almost certainly had its sources in the emerging interests and experiences of the Dunravens, stimulated by Continental travel and a sturdy purse.

Preceding pages: *The Dunraven family's interest in Irish medieval architecture is evident in the Gothic style of the house and the early Hiberno-Romanesque details of the vestibule.*

These pages: *Rossmore's published* (right) *and unpublished* (above) *views of the great hall, with the 'minstrel's gallery' piercing the arcade, based on a Continental example seen by the Dunravens on their travels in the 1830s. The chimney-piece is by Pugin.*

If the hall is the most complex space, the most dramatic is the gallery, a huge timber-roofed space rising through two storeys and stretching nearly forty-five metres. With its architectural details, pictures and furnishings, the idea, as Cornforth so well expressed it, was to 'create 250 years of history overnight'. The family history from the twelfth century is traced in Willement's stained glass and portraits – both family heirlooms and acquisitions – which carry the story through in more intimate, if also more vague terms. Seventeenth-century Flemish stalls, purchased by the Dunravens during their Continental tour of 1834–36, add to the ambiguous combination of old and new.

It may have been the 3rd Earl who introduced Pugin, for he was an Oxford movement convert to Catholicism, and Pugin was the most vociferous proponent of Catholic medieval architecture. Pugin himself recorded the provision of drawings for the hall ceiling, staircase and fireplace, as well as for the dining room, library and terrace, but his archaeological correctness could never control the vivid imaginations evident in the overall planning of the building. So, despite visiting the house, he did little more than influence details of the work.

It was Pugin's successor, the English architect P. C. Hardwick, who developed the next and final major phase of work at Adare. This involved the laying out of the surrounding terraces, and the completion of the southern range, that which looks across to the river and occupies the site of the original classical house. Although Hardwick's work embodies the professional finish of the later nineteenth century, it possesses none of the amateur exuberance of the earlier work. Yet his patron, the 3rd Earl, was to establish himself as one of the foremost authorities on Irish antiquities. He was a friend of the celebrated Irish antiquary George Petrie, and collated the material for the posthumously published *Notes on Irish Antiquities*, one of the most significant antiquarian publications of the century.

Adare Manor continued *Country Life*'s interest in the distinctive character of Ireland's Gothic revival, and it was one of the few buildings from the western part of Ireland to appear in its pages in the 1960s. In 1969, at the time of its coverage, its future looked bright, as it was being reoccupied, after a period of vacancy, by the 6th Earl of Dunraven. Unfortunately, despite the huge contribution by the family to the development of Irish studies in the nineteenth century, in the absence of any wider support the endeavour failed and the house was sold, converted to a hotel and its contents dispersed.

The gallery, shown here before its contents were dispersed. Some forty-five metres long and with full-height oriels looking to the river beyond, it was among the most impressive of interiors in Ireland.

SEVENTEEN

BALLYFIN

Co LAOIS

Even into the 1970s *Country Life* continued to play a central role in the publication of new Irish scholarship in architectural history. The discovery by the Knight of Glin of papers concerning one of Ireland's most impressive classical houses, Ballyfin in Co. Laois, enabled Dr Edward McParland to clarify the unexpectedly complex history of the building as part of his wider studies of the main architects responsible for the design, Richard and William Vitruvius Morrison, the father-and-son practice dominating domestic Irish architecture in the 1820s.

Ballyfin, at the edges of the Slieve Bloom mountains in the central midlands of Ireland, is an estate that appears, falsely, to be naturally distinguished by the kind of undulating landscape that Capability Brown tried to create.

In fact, it was moulded to enhance the setting, not least by the builder of house, Charles Henry Coote, 9th Baronet. Coote purchased the estate from William Wellesley-Pole, a brother of the Duke of Wellington. Wellesley-Pole had added his suffix in honour of the Poles who had held the estate since the seventeenth century and from whom, as distant cousin, William had inherited in about 1780.

Though with the estate then apparently somewhat encumbered by debt, Wellesley-Pole was able to secure its finances and continue improvements already initiated by the Poles, so that by the opening of the new century he could boast, for example, one of the largest deer parks in Ireland and 'the only place in the country where the breed of pigs was … improved'. However by 1812, with the marriage of his son to an English heiress, and his continuing unpopularity as a figure in government, he put the estate on the market and removed himself to England.

Charles Coote, who also traced his Irish ancestry to the seventeenth century, took advantage of the opportunity to purchase and, ultimately, to improve the estate at Ballyfin. Coote probably completed the purchase in about 1814, the year of his marriage, and immediately set about the development of its six hundred acres. Such work, carried out with the assistance of a Mr Sutherland, included the refining of its contours, 'to ensure a gently undulating surface', the development of the 'farmery', and a tower one hundred and thirty feet tall from which one might see, reputedly, sixteen counties – presumably on a clear day.

Preceding pages: *The house, showing the small part designed in about 1821 by the little-known architect Dominic Madden, with the conservatory, added in about 1850, in an unpublished photograph by Gibson.*

These pages: *An unpublished view of the central gallery* (above) *situated behind the starkly classical entrance hall* (right) *and flanked by the staircase hall, in the distance, and the rotunda, unseen. The rich plasterwork and columnar screen recall the dining room at Carton.*

It was known, not least through the efficient self-promotion of the Morrisons themselves, that they were called in by Coote to provide him with a suitable new house. However, it was only the investigation of family papers by the Knight of Glin that uncovered the involvement in earlier work of a rather less famous architect, Dominic Madden. Madden is one of the many Irish architects of undoubted ability whose practice has received little attention from historians. His talent is confirmed by his success at the Catholic cathedral of Tuam, Co. Galway, the best of the three cathedral churches linked with his name, and his practice appears to have been associated largely with Roman Catholic patrons in the centre and west of Ireland. How he gained the commission from Coote is unclear, but documents show that in 1821 Madden presented an estimate of £23,501 for the proposed new house, and in 1822 claimed the standard five per cent fee on the £6,314 worth of work then finished. Evidently almost a third of the work on Madden's design had been completed before Coote turned to the more prominent practice of Richard Morrison and son.

McParland's analysis of the house and papers, in the light of these new discoveries, allowed him to compose a more complete history of the building. He was able to suggest that the top-lit rotunda and bowed library were the remnants of the scheme originally devised by Madden. That this arrangement repeated a layout found in a neighbouring great house with which Coote certainly would have been familiar, Emo Court by James Gandon, suggested the combined activities of a dominant patron and an able architect lacking, perhaps, in persuasive talents.

In addition to Madden's work, the Morrisons employed the progressive neoclassical detailing that distinguished their work in this period. As a result of his study of the firm, McParland was able to clarify the different responsibilities of the two Morrisons. Richard had already established himself as an architect of significance by the opening of the nineteenth century, having schooled himself in an Irish neoclassicism deriving from Gandon, William Chambers's Casino in Dublin, and James Wyatt's country houses. Austerity, combined with occasional dramatic spatial effects and a latter-day enthusiasm for Palladio on the one hand, and Stuart and Revett's delineations of Greek antiquities on the other, distinguished his fundamentally light manner.

Left and above: The top-lit rotunda, also a room surviving from Madden's arrangement, became in the Morrisons' scheme an anteroom to the library, reached from the central saloon. Madden's source may have been a similar eighteenth-century arrangement by James Gandon at nearby Emo Court.

Richard Morrison's son and eventual professional partner, William Vitruvius Morrison, received a more aggressively international education, in keeping with the ambitions of his father and the interests of the day. Visiting the Continent in 1821, and travelling to Rome and Greece, he improved his archaeological scholarship, familiarized himself with contemporary manners, and returned to Ireland with a first-hand experience of current Continental taste for heavier ornament and greater elaboration.

Ballyfin presents a coherent whole, and it is not easy to distinguish between the work of father and son, especially as contemporary reports on the work are often contradictory and, on occasion, misleading. William's biographer, his brother John, credited the younger architect with the design 'whilst in partnership with his father'. This apparently decisive statement conflicts with Richard's signing of the majority of the drawings, and Coote's own contemporary reports which confirm the father's leading role in the new work. Yet, in the absence of evidence to the contrary, McParland was able to attribute features of the house to one or the other architect on the basis of style. According to him, the majority of the decorative finishes are by William Vitruvius, but Richard appears to have organized the final layout, based on Madden's work, developing a central sequence of bowed library, rotunda, saloon and staircase hall, all arranged in enfilade. This arrangement is preceded by a stark entrance hall, enhancing further the drama of what is to come, in a manner typical of the spatial dynamism of Richard's style.

The house survived well throughout the nineteenth century, the most important addition being the superb conservatory – one of the finest domestic examples in these islands – added in about 1850 to the rear of the house. It was probably constructed after designs by the famous Irish engineer Richard Turner, who designed similar structures in the Botanic Gardens at Dublin and, with Decimus Burton, Kew, both recently restored in recognition of their importance.

With the arrival of the twentieth century, Ballyfin's fortunes, and those of the family, became more mixed. On the death of Algernon, 12th Baronet, in 1920, his son, Ralph, had to relinquish the expensive house and live in a smaller pre-war house on the estate. In 1923 the family moved to Dublin, selling the estate to the Land Commission, from which the house eventually passed into the care of the Patrician Brothers to be used as a school.

EIGHTEEN

GLENSTAL CASTLE

Co LIMERICK

Some Irish houses find it hard to live up to expectations. Glenstal Castle, situated beside the Tipperary border of Co. Limerick, originally had its tremendous aspirations undermined first by economy and then by the practical needs of a country house. In its present role as a boys' school run by the Benedictine order, modern buildings encroach sharply on its setting and undermine its grandiose designs. Even with this conflict of ambition and function, the castle remains one of the most magnificent attempts at creating an Irish version of the medieval Anglo-Norman castle. Yet Glenstal's castle-like form is not due to the need for defence. In a tradition going back to Georgian castles such as Glin, Co. Limerick, and Charleville Forest, Co. Offaly, the intention is to evoke some ancient time, but combined with the needs of a modern country house.

The appearance of antiquity also might give to its patron at least the suggestion of an ancient lineage, and that in itself, in an increasingly disjointed Irish society, was not without significance. The Barringtons settled in Limerick relatively late, at the end of the seventeenth century, and furthered their fame less through marriage than through hard work, innovative industry and successful trading. Professional advancement was not accompanied by significant social advance, and though Joseph Barrington was a baronet, the family were in essence business people rather than aristocracy. Although there was no speedier way of securing the impression of title and history than by having one's own castle, his son Matthew, Crown Solicitor for Munster, must have recognized the discomfort of real castles, and so decided to build a more comfortable, modern version.

The design passed through numerous phases even before building began. Even after construction commenced in 1838, from designs provided by the successful English architect William Bardwell, changes, indecision and economic variables all added further complications. Initially, before the selection of the design, the problem was the choice of site. Not having inherited lands on which to build, Barrington might use any site, and he decided first on property he had leased in 1818 from the increasingly encumbered Limerick estates of the Lords Carbery. Part of these included the district of Glenstal, at one time intended as a site for the house, and although Barrington later turned to various other sites, he took with him the name. Consequently, in a very characteristic Georgian incongruity, the title of this apparently ancient castle bears no relation to the lands on which it sits.

During the protracted development of the designs Barrington advanced his professional career and, with that, his ambitions for his new castle. He turned first to local architects, James and George Richard Paine, both Englishmen trained under John Nash and settled in Ireland, who had an established practice in country-house castles. James was already involved with the Dunravens at Adare, perhaps endearing him further to Barrington. Less familiar was the second figure selected at this early stage, William O'Hara of Dublin. His practice had little prestige, though his proposal to create an Irish Windsor at Glenstal may well have captured Barrington's imagination. However, neither practice could entirely satisfy him, so he turned to London for further ideas, approaching first Decimus Burton, selected perhaps because of his work on the Phoenix Park in Dublin. Somehow he also made contact with William Bardwell, the architect finally selected for the project.

Bardwell, little known today despite his long life – he died in 1890 aged ninety-five – was still less familiar when first employed by Barrington, and Glenstal remains his most important work. After training in England he advanced his studies, rather unusually for the date, in France. He gained some celebrity through competing both for the London Houses of Parliament and for the Fitzwilliam Museum at Cambridge. It may well have been the Norman tower proposed by Bardwell as his entrance to Parliament that suggested him to his Limerick patron, though as all periods of architecture were intended to be represented in that building, any prospective client might have found something of interest.

The ultimate inspiration for Bardwell's Glenstal lay less with the designs of the Paines or O'Hara than with the work of Thomas Hopper, notably his Gosford Castle in Armagh, of 1819. This was the first Norman revival castle in these islands, and the first in a style that Hopper would make his own. Neither Barrington nor Bardwell need have been familiar with Gosford itself, for by the late 1830s the type was not uncommon. In any case, Bardwell provided a competent and efficient design, full of striking first impressions and suitable economies, not least through prescribing the construction of only part of this apparently quadrangular castle. Once again Georgian incongruity is in evidence, though by 1838 we have left that period behind and entered the era of Victoria.

Bardwell was in Ireland in 1840, reviewing the completed work. It then extended from the largest, southern, tower to the gatehouse in the south-east wall. However, work stopped in the following year, and began again only in 1846 or 1847. Construction paused again in 1849, to recommence in about 1853, with Bardwell finally paid off, and a Cork architect, Joshua Hargrave, appointed to complete the work with restricted funds, and to create something approaching a functioning building. Inevitably, pragmatic decisions were required, and the dream first envisaged by Barrington could not be realized. One hopes he was not too disappointed that the final work failed to live up to his original expectations, because although the castle has many moments that do not fulfil, it also

Preceding pages: The entrance range, with Gibson's unpublished view of the drawing-room fireplace surmounted by frames after Iffley church, another noted example of the Hiberno-Romanesque revival.

These pages: Gibson's views of the Norman revival portal (above) and the vista through a long sequence of doorways (right), convincingly misaligned and with the staircase seen on the left, were both unpublished.

The central pier in the library (top centre) *has two chimney-pieces back to back, with a cluster of columns rising to carry the plain ribbed vault.*

The austere architecture is relieved by the lively sculptural details (top left and right; bottom left and right), *all effectively suggestive of the Romanesque sources, and probably freely copied from published illustrations of such work.*

The doorcase (above centre) *which links the unfinished dining room and the drawing room was modelled after a late twelfth-century portal in St Flannan's Cathedral, Killaloe, Co. Clare, one of the greatest expressions of Irish culture.*

In its original form, the features capture well the influence of Viking style, a manner already evident in the Book of Kells of nearly half a millennium earlier, and still surviving in the Norman period. The copy was carved by a local sculptor named White in 1841, and reproduces well the manner of the original, even in its details (above left and right).

possesses a magnificent sense of scale outside and an imaginative combination of traditional Celtic forms inside, together with the occasional set piece that matches the best in any Irish house.

Perhaps the most appealing aspect of Glenstal is the local character of the detailing, a feature possibly deriving more from Bardwell's imagination, or even Hargrave's, than from Barrington's. Most carving was executed by an English firm, W. T. Kelsey of Brompton, which provided fifteen cases of columns, capitals and corbels in 1844. However, the detailing of much of the carved work suggests some familiarity with Irish early Christian sources, and echoes abound of recent work at Adare Manor, itself being slowly built over many years, although using native craftsmen.

If much of the carved detail is evocative rather than accurate, there are also striking and significant copies of Irish early Christian design. The style was then only beginning to receive proper attention as a part of Ireland's heritage. The idea may have been inspired again by the Dunravens' Adare – Barrington is known to have had business dealings with the family – for they used such Hiberno-Romanesque designs in the doorcases of their entrance hall. At Glenstal we find superb copies, notably the doorcase connecting the dining room and the drawing room. This is a magnificently carved and surprisingly accurate reconstruction of the doorway in Killaloe Cathedral, Co. Clare, today recognized as one of the masterpieces of the Irish Romanesque. A lack of

understanding of the importance of such work was prevalent in mid-nineteenth-century Ireland – it might be compared to the recent lack of interest in the heritage of the country house – and its introduction here was an important moment in the history of the revival of interest in Ireland's Christian and Celtic legacy.

It was as part of a wider interest in Ireland's national character that the future of this important house was put in jeopardy. The tragic accidental shooting of the daughter of the 5th Baronet, Charles Barrington, by the IRA in an ambush on the Black and Tans in May 1921, led to the family's departure and, eventually, the sale of the estate in 1925. Fortunately, the castle was bought by Monsignor James Ryan, and taken over by the Benedictines of Maredsous, Belgium, who through the influence of an Irish abbot had developed the idea of establishing an Irish house. In 1927 the first monk arrived, and Glenstal became an abbey in 1957, succeeding also in establishing itself as one of the most famous Irish schools, and certainly the one with the most convincing castle.

Above left: *Outside, the solid architectural mood of the figurative sculpture, only partly distinguished from its columnar origins, gives to this part of the castle a convincing solidity.*

Above right: *The irregular vaulting in the library captures a rare monumental character inside the castle, here unhampered by painting the vaults blue with gilded stars.*

NINETEEN

LISSADELL

Co SLIGO

Lissadell, home of the Gore-Booths, is on the north-western seaboard of Ireland, in the northerly extremes of Co. Sligo and in the centre of what has become popularly, if somewhat misleadingly, known as 'Yeats country'. The association of Sligo with Ireland's most prominent artistic family, the Yeatses, springs first from a link with Lissadell, as Susan Pollexfen, wife of John Butler Yeats, and mother of William, the poet, and Jack, the painter, was a friend of the Gore-Booths. The Gore-Booths, however, played a role in Ireland's history that was very much their own.

It was William Butler Yeats's friendship with two daughters of the Gore-Booth family, Constance and Eva Selena, that inspired his especially close association with Lissadell.

The sisters possessed the intuitive artistic personalities beloved of Yeats, supplemented with revolutionary interests in nationalism and the suffragette movement. After he had visited the family in 1894–5, they won from him the modest compliment that they were 'very pleasant, kindly, inflammable ... ever ready to take up new ideas and new things'.

The Gore-Booths can trace their Irish ancestry to the early seventeenth century and the arrival of Paul Gore, whose son, Francis, settled at Ardtermon Castle, which is now a ruin. His grandson, Nathaniel, married Letitia Booth, whose name and substantial fortune, derived from estates in northern England, he brought to the family. It was their son, Both, who was created 1st Baronet in 1760. Robert, 4th Baronet, called on the services of the English architect Francis Goodwin to build a new house. This must have occurred in about 1830 as tenders dated 1831 survive, submitted by the English contractor James Nowell, of Dewsbury, Yorkshire; his second tender of £11,701 appears to have been successful. The new house was intended to replace the Georgian house as the family seat, situated even closer to the Atlantic coastline, which had in its turn replaced the old castle of Ardtermon.

Goodwin's successful northern English practice may well have recommended his services to Robert, for he had already secured fame with his completion of the Manchester Town Hall and Assembly Rooms. Furthermore, in 1833 his submission, by invitation, of designs for new Houses of Parliament in London that were then under consideration, were described as 'the best of those sent in'. Two years later, the actual destruction of the Houses of Parliament by fire led to a new competition, one for which Goodwin, naturally, had high hopes. However, while working on his proposals for the competition, he overexerted himself, which led to insomnia, apoplexy and, on 30 August 1830, death. Lissadell remains the finest testimony to his abilities as a domestic architect, if also to his limitations.

The house itself forms, outside at least, a stark Grecian counterpoint to the harsh winds of its Atlantic seaboard setting and the rugged lines of the surrounding mountains. Long pilaster strips, or *antae*, rise to a tall, bald entablature. Unenlivened by either ornament or roof lines, the structure has the hard honesty of a child's building block. Simple horizontal bands tie the entire composition together. The kitchens and related services are in the basement, allowing the house to remain starkly isolated from its

surroundings; a tunnel connects the submerged kitchen yard to the stables beyond, as at Caledon.

At one end of the building, a bow breaks forward to give more generous vistas towards the majestic surroundings, though as if to dispense with any frivolity it is given an additional parapet. At the other end, the northern, the pedimented centre breaks forward to allow for the creation of a *porte-cochère*, a necessary luxury in a district that might take the full brunt of the Atlantic storms. Neither the pocket of the patron – who used local Ballysadare limestone – nor the taste of the architect, suggest any further inclination to enrich the exterior. It is significant that when Yeats writes of the house, it is its setting and views that impress him, rather than its form:

The light of evening, Lissadell,
Great windows open to the south ...

Inside the building both architect and patron happily have relaxed, and behind the door under the *porte-cochère*, the building opens out from its abstract austerity to become a house and, in every sense of the word, a home. For the more observant, some sense of that change of mood might be gained from the deep concave recess framing the entrance door. Inside, the visitor is caught first by a sequence of vistas that suggest – at least if all the doors are opened – a destruction of the material of the architecture in favour of the expression of space.

To the right, the billiard room is strewn with stuffed animals, as though Dali were expected for dinner. To the left, and framed between deceptively thin Doric columns, the staircase stretches ahead in the first flight of its imperial rise. Above, the ceiling is removed, as vistas are created to first-floor galleries through Ionic columns matching, in arrangement, the Doric below. Ahead, a view may be gained of the gallery, columnar and magnificent, stretching into the distance, its curved and pilastered termination almost suggestive of infinity. From this point, the zenith of the building's spatial character, Goodwin's genius in the efficient design of domestic architecture is well displayed. This is especially striking

Preceding pages: *The entrance front, in neo-Grecian manner, with the bow drawing room projecting on the left, and the reception rooms extending across the southern front hiding the full-height gallery, here seen from one end.*

These pages: *The entrance hall and Kilkenny marble staircase* (right) *form an exciting and unexpected contrast to the geometry of the exterior, and join the first-floor lobby* (above)*, with its exercise in taxidermy further softening the lines, seen here in an unpublished view by Gibson.*

as, other than in his treatment of the space, the actual arrangement is not especially unusual.

In the gallery, it is clear that Goodwin's need to impress, the same that caused his death, has led him here to overestimate his abilities. Giant orders surround a space terminating at either end in semicircular recesses. To one side, an Ionic screen of columns set inside the line of the wall gives a suggestion of a space beyond. However, this is undermined by the solid wall immediately behind, one not even pierced by windows, as had been intended originally, because it would have connected to the kitchen court.

The rest of the gallery walls are given more of the sharp *antae* reminiscent of the exterior, if here more deeply projecting. Though they enliven the surface, they do little else to serve this grand interior, and the top-lighting and windows over the columns

Left: *The drawing room, situated beside the library, has a columnar screen inset into the wall, continuing the architectural manner of the gallery, if on a more human scale.*

Above: *The dining room with its quirky murals by Casimir Markievicz, Constance's husband. Sarah Purser's portrait of Constance and Eva as children, in the woods at Lissadell, hangs over the fireplace.*

contribute significantly to a space that is, in every other way, most imposing. The room's large scale, rising the full height of the house, impresses despite Godwin's uncertainty over what to do with his orders, and even Yeats acknowledged its success as a 'great sitting room as high as a church'.

In the succeeding rooms, in effect the more ordinary living rooms, Goodwin returns to a more domestic scale and character. The library – now the bow drawing room – the drawing room, anteroom and dining room lead off one another in succession around the core of the gallery. Throughout these rooms Goodwin relishes the contrast of sharp geometry and extravagant chimney-pieces. Such severity was softened by the generous intelligence of the long succession of residents and visitors.

Today the abundant taxidermy, soft furnishings and exquisite paintings all lend the severe building a more relaxed, convivial Irish mood, an atmosphere that has always characterized the history of the house. Sir Robert mortgaged the estate to feed his tenants during the Famine of the 1840s, and his son was equally renowned for his generosity. The house and its contents are still in the care of the family.

TWENTY

BIRR CASTLE

Co OFFALY

A visit to Birr Castle, home of the Earls of Rosse since 1619, and the town sidling up against it, is one of the most enchanting experiences to be had in Ireland. One finds here a summation of Irish country house histories. First spurred by dramatic confrontations in the seventeenth century, then eased by the political distractions of the eighteenth century and the more passive scientific and philanthropic concerns of the nineteenth, Birr stands today as a triumphant representative of the cultural and historical interests of the family.

The history of the castle of Birr begins at the end of the sixteenth century with the arrival in Ireland of two brothers, William and Laurence Parsons. It was the younger brother, Laurence, Attorney General for Munster from 1612, who in 1619–20 acquired some fourteen hundred acres in a fertile and sheltered part of central Ireland known as Ely O'Carroll, the lands of the O'Carrolls.

Among the O'Carrolls' fortifications to come with the territory was a huge square tower near the present castle. This was known as the Black Castle, and it was here that Laurence, by then titled, established his seat.

From 1620, and in acknowledgement of the dangerous times still ahead for Ireland, Parsons began upgrading the fortifications, the most significant development being the construction – or reconstruction – of the gatehouse. It was this structure, the entrance to the original castle complex, that was to become the core of the modern Birr Castle. Intriguingly, and revealing the remarkable imagination in the reuse of old buildings that seems to carry through the whole history of Irish country houses, the present hall was the first-floor room over the original arched entrance, now located at basement level.

Clear evidence of the detailed form of other medieval work in the present castle is minimal, but it would appear that the entrance was framed by two diagonally placed towers or flankers, projecting forward and providing protection for the gateway. Parsons also extended the outbuildings, adding stables and a kitchen wing. These were swept away in their entirety in about 1778 by a descendant, Sir William Parsons, who wanted more freedom in the laying out of his new gardens, in a style inspired by, if rather less inventive than, Capability Brown's Italianate manner.

Details of the arrangement of the former castle remain unclear due to later works. The fabric of the gate tower was gradually overlaid through numerous accretions, and largely re-formed, most notably by the addition of Georgian Gothic details. These alterations enabled it to remain the principal residence, much as had been the case with Howth Castle, so forgoing the alternative

Preceding pages: The entrance front, seen from the nineteenth-century Vaubanesque fortifications, and the Georgian Gothic saloon inside.

These pages: Views to and from the meandering River Camcor, showing the suspension bridge erected before 1826 by the then Lord Oxmantown, later the 3rd Earl, and among the earliest of its type to survive.

of building anew. As at Howth too, at Birr the irregular and romantic outline that one sees today represents the continuing importance of the earlier fabric in the modern layout.

As might be expected in seventeenth-century Ireland, Parsons's tower had much to endure before the more settled times of the eighteenth and nineteenth centuries. In the turmoil of the 1640s in particular, Birr, no less than Ireland at large, suffered greatly, being besieged, burned, deserted and recaptured. It was after this that the gatehouse began to adopt its modern role as a residence, a change testified by the construction of one of Ireland's most important surviving pieces of carpentry, the open-well yew staircase.

This rises in broad flights with low steps through three storeys of the present castle. It was even famous in its own day, for the English topographer Thomas Dineley reported in his journal that it was spoken of as 'the fairest staircase in Ireland'. If this report comes at second hand, it only emphasizes the renown of this work. The monumental proportions of its robust details, in conjunction with its light, open flights, make it a remarkable feat of design and construction in its own right. It has, however, been reconstructed in part, as it was damaged by a fire in the building that occurred on 25 June 1832.

Above: *The entrance hall takes its shape from its original role as the room over the arched entrance to the castle, giving it the distinctive elongated proportion. Its detailing is, of course, nineteenth century.*

Right: *The saloon was created by Laurence Parsons, later 2nd Earl of Rosse, in 1801, with the assistance of the architect–builder John Johnston. The architectural forms are picked out in white and gold, confirming the rococo Gothic conception of the room.*

The castle was besieged again in the 1690s, at great human and economic cost, and to the detriment of the building itself. The gatehouse survived, and underwent limited development in the ensuing period. Indeed, after the turmoil of the previous century the 1700s must have provided some relief to the family. However, as they received only minimal recompense for their support of successful claimants to the throne in the previous century, they were not so much in need of a completely fashionable fabric. Instead they respected and developed their existing resources, the castle, estate and surroundings, with, as ever, exemplary care.

It was characteristics such as these – conscientiousness, humanity and benevolence – that distinguished the family's future activities. At the end of the century, before the dissolution of the Irish Parliament, political and social duties centred on the promotion

of Irish autonomy occupied the family. Consequently, only minor alterations were effected inside. The evidence of the family's continuing concern as landlords remains well evident even today. The town of Birr, or Parsonstown as it was formerly known, remains one of the most appealing examples of Irish urban design.

In the nineteenth century, new interests seized the castle's residents. Retiring from the futile distraction of the political morass of post-Union Ireland, and having seen his father, William, instigate the development of the famous gardens, Sir Laurence Parsons, displaying in abundance characteristic energies and intellectual curiosity, turned his attentions to the development of the castle. Though he was to inherit the title of Lord Rosse from his uncle, a half-brother to his father, and become 2nd Earl of Rosse in 1806, his failure to inherit his uncle's huge fortune probably ensured that work could be no more than a partial remodelling.

The 2nd Earl called on the services of a little-known local architect or builder, John Johnston, apparently no relation to the architect Francis Johnston. The Earl himself appears to have taken on the task of determining the rearrangement of the medieval gatehouse as a seat proper to his title, and in about 1801 he

Left: *The staircase must have been constructed some time between the Restoration and 1681. Made of yew – Dineley reports on the plentiful supply of this timber in the region – its massive proportions are characteristic of the period. It was reconstructed after a fire in 1832, but the main features are original.*

Above: *The benevolent care of the family also promoted the development of the estate workshops, and these are credited with the curious style of the bedroom created for the new wife of the 3rd Earl in 1836.*

prepared a series of sketches in a notebook which records projects and ideas for the new work. As might be guessed, all of this was Gothic, in acknowledgement of the historic character of the surviving work. This may well signify an awareness of the increasing interest in medieval design evidenced already in the building of Charleville Forest, not far away in the same county.

Rosse, assisted in some undefined way by his architect Johnston, created the central porch and its great arch largely in the form that is seen today. The intention, as Girouard observes, may have been to disguise the lack of balance between the sides, but equally it provides further variety in the massing of the castle. The fire of 1832 that damaged the staircase also led to the remodelling of this section of the front. In its original form it rose only two storeys above ground, surmounted by a steep pitched roof possibly of pre-Georgian origin. Rosse replaced this with the present top storey and finished the skyline with the double-stepped battlements similar to those at Charleville Forest.

One major early nineteenth-century addition is the elegant plaster-vaulted Gothic saloon. With the slim lines of its wall shafts and ribs, the free flow of the window tracery and the curious irregular octagon of its plan, the room possesses all the light, airy mood of the best of later Georgian Gothic, and remains one of Birr's finest interiors.

The 2nd Earl also carried out extensive decoration inside the castle, mostly in a style rather heavier than the saloon, and one that, by the time of execution in the later 1830s, looked to a more robust, Victorian taste. The dining room especially, but also the entrance hall, suggest this new mood, still hardly archaeological, but no longer aspiring to the prettiness of the earlier work.

Through much of the 1800s, science rather than architecture preoccupied the Rosses. Their celebrated astronomical observations left the gardens with their most surprising folly, the battlemented support for the largest reflecting telescope in the world. Members of the family also studied engineering – the brother of the 4th Earl, Sir Charles Algernon Parsons, helped develop the steam turbine. This, in combination with their conscientious awareness of wider responsibilities, secured the future of the estate in the family's hands to the present generation.

The gardens at Birr are among the most famous in Ireland, and have been developed over many generations, notably in this century when the 6th Earl and his wife created the baroque effect in their ribbed hornbeam hedge walks (above) and the part-pruned lines of three-hundred-year-old giant box trees (right).

Achill Island 8–9
Adam, Robert 15, 16, 55, 113
Adam, William 113
Adare Manor 55, 158–163, 169, 175
Annesley, 5th Earl of 10
Annesley, Countess 21
Ardtermon Castle 178
Astonbury 23
Avary Tipping, H. 15

Balawley Park 23
Ball, Elrington 12
Ballyfin 80, 164–169
Bardwell, William 172, 175
Bartoli, Dominic 99
Beaulieu 18, 23, 126–133, 160
Beckford, William 139
Beit, Sir Alfred 83, 91
Beleek Manor 7, 11, 21
Belgard Castle 18, 23
Belmore, Earls of 93, 94, 99
Belvedere House 135
Bence-Jones, Mark 20, 61
Berkeley, Bishop 69
Bindon, Francis 87
Birr Castle 18, 182–191
Boehm, Sir Joseph Edgar 149
Boom Hall 102
Botanic Gardens, Glasnevin 17, 23, 169
Briscoe House 8
Brooks, James 155
Brown, Lancelot 'Capability' 76, 79, 165, 185
Buckingham House 52
Burgh, Thomas 11, 71
Burlington, Lord 15, 71, 113
Burn, William 11
Burton, Decimus 169, 172
Butler, Eleanor 17
Butler, R.M. 17

Cahircon (or Cahiracon) 10
Caledon 16, 17, 100–107, 178
Carton 15, 16, 74–81, 85, 87, 88
Castle, Richard 16, 75–76, 83, 87, 111, 115
Castlecoole 16, 92–99, 120, 123
Castletown (Co. Kildare) 15, 16, 20, 25, 49, 52, 64–73, 85, 88, 120, 141
Castletown Cox 12, 14, 20, 21, 23, 46–55
Castlewellan 10–11, 21
Chambers, William 15, 94, 102, 169
Charleville Forest 18, 134–141, 171, 190
Chequers 23

Clearwell Court 52
Clontra 18
Conolly, James 160
Cooley, Thomas 101, 102, 104, 106, 123, 124
Cornforth, John 7, 10, 12, 14, 20, 21, 65, 88, 91, 160
Country Life history 7–25; photography 20–25
Cox, Michael (Archbishop of Cashel, formerly Bishop of Ossory) 49–51
Craig, Maurice 4, 12, 17–18, 20, 65
Curraghmore 5, 94, 142–149

Dickinson, P.L. 14, 57, 61, 128
Dineley, Thomas 186
Donoghue, Michael 160
Dublin Airport 17
Dublin Castle 139
Duckart, Davis (Daviso D'Arcort) 12, 20, 47, 51–52

Elliot, Robert 14
Elton Hall 16
Emo Court 169
Eyrecourt 128

Farnham, Lord 10
Ffranckfort Castle 21
FitzGerald, Brian 15, 79, 83, 88
FitzGerald, Desmond 17
Fonthill Abbey 139

Galilei, Alessandro 69, 71
Gandon, James 15, 17, 58, 79, 97, 101, 169
Georgian Society Records 12, 14, 16, 23, 51, 52, 55, 57, 73, 91, 109, 113, 143
Gibson, Jonathan 23, 25, 91
Gill, Arthur 23, 115
Gill, Macdonald 38
Girouard, Mark 18–20, 25, 127, 128, 130, 133, 135, 141, 143, 149, 155, 190
Glenstal Castle 170–175
Glin 25, 171
Glin, Knight of 12, 20, 47, 52, 65, 113, 160, 165, 169
Glover, John 124
Goodwood House 102
Gosford Castle 172
Gow, Ian 10
Gray of Chelsea 11
Griffin, David 69
Guinness, Desmond 20, 65, 73

Hall, Michael 7, 10

Hargrave, Joshua 172, 175
Haughton, John 76
Headfort 15, 16
Henson, A.E. 21–23, 25, 55, 57, 58, 91, 104, 106
Henson, Maudie 21
Heywood 12–13, 20, 21, 47, 56–63
Holkham Hall 139
Holy Island 21
Hopper, Thomas 172
Howth Castle 12, 15, 36–45, 57, 185
Hudson, Edward 7, 21, 23, 25
Humewood Castle 18, 150–157
Hussey, Christopher 10, 14, 16, 17, 18, 20, 23, 27, 29, 30, 43, 65, 94, 97, 99, 101, 104, 106, 109, 111, 115, 119, 120, 123, 127, 128
Hussey-Walsh, V. 9, 21

Irish Architectural Archive 4, 69, 124, 136
Irish Georgian Society 18, 20, 25, 65, 73
Ivory, Thomas 79

Jackson-Stops, Gervase 99
Jekyll, Gertrude 35, 61
Johnston, Francis 16, 79–80, 119, 120, 123, 124, 136, 139, 141, 189
Johnston, John 189, 190
Johnston, Richard 58, 97–99
Jourdain, Margaret 15, 17

Kelsey, W.T. 175
Kent, William 139
Killaloe Cathedral 175
Kimberley, Albert 152
Knox, W.G. 21
Knox-Gore, P. and S. 21

Lafranchini family 16, 71, 88
Lambay 12, 13, 15, 20, 23, 26–35, 37, 57, 61
Landaff, Earl of 8
Lawrence, Sir Thomas 106
Lewis, Samuel 29
Lindsay, Norah 52
Lismore Castle 23
Lissadell 176–181
Lucan House 16
Lutyens, Edwin 12, 13, 15, 20, 23, 27, 30, 33, 35, 37, 38, 41, 43, 44, 52, 57, 58, 61, 63

Madden, Dominic 169
Magdalen College Chapel, Oxford 141

Malahide Castle 16
Mallaby-Deeley, Sir Henry 80
Maude, Alice 8–9
Maxwell, Constantia 17
Mayo, Lady 12
McParland, Edward 18, 20, 165, 169
Montgomery, Maria and Sidney 130
Moore, Christopher 80
Morris, Roger 139
Morrison, Richard 79–80, 165, 169
Morrison, William Vitruvius 165, 169
Mount Stewart 15
Moyne Abbey 8

Nash, John 102, 104, 106, 172
Nowell, James 178
Nowlan, John 51

O'Hara, William 172
O'Malley, Grace 8, 41–43
Onslow, Lady 8, 20, 21, 41
Orange, William of 133
Osborne, Patrick 51, 55

Paine, George Richard 172
Paine, James 160, 172
Palladio, Andrea 113, 169
Pearce, Sir Edward Lovett 16, 69, 71, 73, 115, 123
Pennethorne, James 106
Phoenix Park, Dublin 172
Playfair, James 16, 123–124
Pococke, Bishop 87
Poë, Sir Hutcheson 21, 63
Pollexfen, Susan 177
Powerscourt 8, 16, 20, 21, 23, 83, 108–117, 149
Powerscourt, Lord 8, 10
Preston, John and Nathaniel 99
Priestly, Michael 102
Pugin, A.W.N. 160

Redwood 136
Rembrandt 91
Richardson, Sir Albert 15
Riley, Charles Ruben 73
Roberts, John 144
Roberts, S.A. 143, 149
Robertson, Daniel 115, 149
Rodanstown 69
Rolleston, T.W. 21
Roper, Lanning 4
Rose, Joseph 99
Rossmore, Lord 23, 160

Rothery, Seán 23
Rowan, Alistair 20
Royal Hospital, Kilmainham 128
Russborough 15, 16, 20, 82–91, 123
Ryder, Thomas 73

Sadleir, Thomas U. 14, 16, 57, 61, 128
Saunders-Knox-Gore, Mathilda 7, 8
Smith, Charles 143, 147
Smythson, Robert 139
Stapleton, Michael 55, 61
Starkey, Alex 25, 149
Stormont 17
Strawberry Hill 136, 139, 141
Sullivan, Sir Edward 11, 12
Swift, Jonathan 102
Swiss Cottage, Cahir 18
Syon House 113

Taylor, G.C. 15, 17
Thomastown Castle 8
Townley Hall 16, 23, 79, 118–125, 136, 139
Trinity College Dublin 11, 124
Tuam Cathedral 169
Tullynally Castle 18, 23
Turner, Richard 169

Ussher, Archbishop James 29

Van der Hagen, Johann 147
Vanbrugh, Sir John 71, 144
Vaux-le-Vicomte, Château of 130
Vermeer, Jan 91
Vernet 91
Verrio 133
Vierpyl, Simon 71

Walpole, Horace 136, 139
Weaver, Sir Lawrence 11–14, 15, 16, 20, 21, 29, 30, 37, 38, 41, 43, 47, 51, 52, 55, 58, 61, 63
Westley F.W. 18, 23, 124, 127, 130
White, William 151, 152, 155, 157
Wollaton Hall 139
Wood, Robert 88, 91
Woodward, Benjamin 18
Wren, Sir Christopher 15
Wyatt, James 16, 79, 94, 99, 139, 147–9, 169

Yeats, W.B. 14, 177, 178, 181